THE ANGEL AND
THE SORCERER

THE ANGEL
AND THE
SORCERER

*The Remarkable Story of the Occult Origins
of Mormonism and the Rise of Mormons
in American Politics*

PETER LEVENDA

IBIS PRESS
Lake Worth, FL

Published in 2012 by Ibis Press
A division of Nicolas-Hays, Inc.
P. O. Box 540206
Lake Worth, FL 33454-0206
www.ibispress.net

Distributed to the trade by
Red Wheel/Weiser, LLC
65 Parker St. • Ste. 7
Newburyport, MA 01950
www.redwheelweiser.com

ISBN 978-0-89254-200-0

Library of Congress Cataloging-in-Publication Data
Available upon request

Book design and production by Studio 31
www.studio31.com

Printed in the United States of America

CONTENTS

INTRODUCTION

As these lines are being written, there is a Mormon running for the Republican Party's nominee for president in the 2012 election. What many people may not realize is that Willard Mitt Romney is not the first Mormon to run for President of the United States.

That honor goes to the founder of Mormonism himself, Joseph Smith Jr.

What many people also may not realize is that Mitt Romney is not the first Mormon to be focused on the acquisition of wealth.

That honor also goes to the founder of Mormonism, Joseph Smith Jr.

In fact, and according to at least one critic, Joseph Smith Jr. was the first real leveraged buyout king, anticipating Mitt Romney's career by at least 150 years.

The story of the origins of the Church of Jesus Christ of Latter-day Saints, more commonly referred to as the LDS Church or simply as the Mormons, is a story of treasure-hunters and sorcerers. This book is not an attempt to denigrate Mormonism or Mormon politicians or presidential candidates, even though the facts presented here may seem at times outrageous or bizarre. This is the real story of a religious denomination that some consider a cult, even a dangerous cult. Since I have written several books that touch on the subject of "religious deviance", I am sensitive to the label "cult" and do not use it lightly. After all, Christianity began as a cult, as a renegade Jewish sect: a spiritual practice observed in secret, in hidden catacombs and Roman cemeteries before it became a state religion in the fourth century CE. One uses the term "cult" at one's peril.

Yet in the case of Mormonism we have a number of factors that drive Evangelical Christians crazy and which arouse suspicion in members of other denominations as well.

For instance, Mormonism's roots in ritual magic. Or its involvement with Freemasonry. The outlawed practice of plural marriage. And the strange practice of the baptism of the dead by which the LDS Church "converts" departed souls of other faiths to Mormonism (presumably without their consent!).

If we deconstruct the history and practices of the LDS Church we gradually come to the realization that what we are seeing is something truly different from contemporary mainstream Christianity. It should be noted that Mormons consider themselves Christians, even though many Christian denominations refuse to extend that designation to the LDS Church. My intention is not to come down on one side or another in that particular debate. What I want to do, however, is make the data available in order to enable a reader who may not be aware of Mormonism's strange history to make an informed decision ... either as a seeker after spiritual knowledge, perhaps considering conversion, or as a voter in an election.

The controversy over John F. Kennedy's candidacy for president is still fresh in my mind, of course. I was only ten years old when he was elected, but the fact that he was a Roman Catholic—as I was born and raised—was a staple of discussions at home and at school. Kennedy was accused of having allegiance to the Vatican rather than to the United States, forcing him to make an impassioned speech in which he made his loyalties clear.

It may be time for Mitt Romney—or for whatever Mormon political contenders may come after him—to consider making the same sort of speech, in order to allay the fears of Evangelicals and others who believe that there is something very unusual about Mormonism.

In the United States, we believe that Church and State are separate. Of course, they are, according to the US Constitution and more specifically the Bill of Rights. But religious feeling and political agendas are often brought together in a single political candidate. We are, after all, human beings and subject to human emotion and psychological conditions. However much we try to compartmentalize our political beliefs and our religious beliefs, in terms of everyday activity the one may wash over into the other. We know this because the political influence of various religious groups is well-known, and reported endlessly in the media.

Ronald Reagan, who is idolized by many on the political Right, was a member of the same religious denomination (the Disciples of Christ) as Jim Jones, the preacher responsible for the Jonestown massacre of 1979. Reagan believed in an impending apocalypse, the End of Days. Jim Jones did his best to bring it on, at least for his followers in the Guyanese jungle where they met their hideous fate. The phrase "drink the Kool-Aid" as a reference to mindlessly following an agenda or a leader comes from the mass murder and suicide at Jonestown where many of the victims were told to drink a cyanide-laced soft drink.

George W. Bush famously told Evangelical Christians that God had told him to run for president.

But Richard Nixon, as the nation's first and so-far only, Quaker president, ignored his religion's pacifist teachings entirely when he ordered the Christmas bombing of Cambodia during the Vietnam War.

What is worse, then, we may ask: a religious zealot as president, or a religious hypocrite?

As the above examples suggest, the answer to this question may depend on the religion. And that is where this conversation about Mormonism must begin. Evangelical Christians, Roman Catholics—and Americans in general—should ask their political candidates (and especially their presidential candidates) whether or not they are true believers in their respective religions. Had Richard Nixon been a true Quaker, it is entirely possible that Cambodia would never have been bombed and that the Vietnam War would have ended years earlier. Had Ronald

Reagan truly believed in the apocalypse and the Second Coming of Jesus, he might have hurried it along with a few well-placed missiles.

If a person running for President of the United States is a true Mormon ... what does that mean for the rest of us?

The author's intention is that this book goes somewhat towards answering that question.

ORIGINS

CHAPTER ONE:

THE SORCERER

Samuel Smith v. Mary Easty.

The deposition of Samuell Smith of Boxford aged about 25 years who testifieth and saith that about five years since I was one night at the house of Isaac Estick [Easty] of Tops-field and I was as far as I know not Rude in discorse and the above said Esticks wife said to me I would not have you be so rude in discorse for I might Rue it here after and as I was agoeing home that night about a quarter of a mile from the said Esticks house by a stone wall I Received a little blow on my shoulder with I know not what and the stone wall rattled very much which affrighted me my horse also was affrighted very much but I cannot give the reason of it.

—*From the Historical Collection of the Topsfield Historical Society concerning the Salem witchcraft trials of 1692*

JOSEPH SMITH, JR. — THE FOUNDER OF MORMONISM—came from a long line of occultists and religious zealots. For instance his ancestor, Samuel Smith, was one of the accusers of Mary Towne Easty who was eventually hanged as a witch at Salem on September 22, 1692. Even his father was well-known as an occultist and exorcist. It should be remembered, however, that Joseph Smith lived in a time and place that was replete with various cults and ceaseless sectarian strife. New prophets were commonplace; new revelations were the subject of endless discussion. There was no single form of Christianity that made it to the shores of the New World in the seventeenth century, but dozens of different denominations some of which spun off even more schismatic groups in the century that followed. Many believers had come to

America to escape various forms of religious persecution in England, France and Germany, from both Protestants and Catholics.

In short, North America was colonized largely by heretics.

This was a different set of circumstances when compared to the southern part of what would become the United States as well as Mexico and Latin America. Colonized by Spain, these were areas subject to Roman Catholic influence and—in some cases, particularly those of the Native American populations—forced conversion. The Holy Inquisition arrived in the Americas under the Spanish sword. Christopher Columbus himself had planned his expedition to what would become the "New World" in order to raise money for a new Crusade against the Islamic forces in Jerusalem, an expedition financed by the King of Spain who in the same year had expelled the last remaining Caliphate from the city of Grenada and who was preparing for an assault on the Holy Land ... an assault that never actually materialized.

Thus religion was a determining factor in the European "discovery" and subsequent colonization of the American continents. The European settlers who have come to represent for many Americans the romantic notion of pious Puritans and quaint Quakers fleeing persecution in their home countries in order to carve out a life of freedom in the New World were, in some instances, religious bigots themselves. While they may have been escaping religious intolerance in Europe, they lost no time in establishing their own intolerant communities of like-minded faithful in the American colonies.

Others, however, were considerably more enlightened. Alchemy and magic were serious topics of discussion and research in seventeenth century America, at least among the intelligentsia. It should be remembered that several members of the Royal Society in England were alchemists, and these would include Elias Ashmole (1617–1692) and Isaac Newton (1642–1727). Ashmole died the year the Salem witchcraft trials began in the colonies; Newton was fifty years old when the trials and subsequent hangings took place. Educated Englishmen who settled in the New England area brought with them the same intellectual pursuits they enjoyed back home, represented by well-stocked libraries of books on alchemy, magic, theology, astrology, and various forms of spiritualism. Indeed, the seventeenth century Governor of Connecticut, John Winthrop Jr, had a personal library that included more than 250 volumes on occult subjects and was a regular correspondent with some of the most famous occult scholars of the day.

Those who were believers in the basic tenets of Christianity found themselves living in a world populated by spirits both good and evil. The Bible is full of accounts of direct contact with the Divine, of prophets and angels, witches and pagan idolators. The Biblical accounts do not deny the possibility of magic and demonolatry; on the contrary, such practices are recognized in order to be condemned. They are not condemned or prohibited because they are superstition or fantasy, but precisely because they work: a person can evoke spirits to visible appearance, as in the case of the Witch of Endor. A person can use divination to determine the will of God and future events, as in the case of the Urim and Thummim. A person can perform magical feats that are astonishing and spectacular, as in the case of Moses versus the Egyptian priests.

And ritual is efficacious and often necessary, as in the many instances of sacrifice and ritual performed at Solomon's Temple, among other examples from both the Old and the New Testaments.

The Protestant Reformation, however, was among other things a critique of the way in which Roman Catholicism interpreted these examples. The ritual of the Mass and of the practices associated with exorcism, healing, etc. were considered degenerate forms of the original Faith. Luther—himself originally a Catholic priest—railed against the inaccessibility of the Bible and the rituals which were available only in the Latin language which meant that only the well-educated could read the Scriptures; this implied that there was a built-in possibility of corruption in the Church, since the priests could represent the Scriptures in any way they chose, secure in the knowledge that the average Catholic could not hope to read the originals anyway. Luther wanted to strip away the institutionalized obfuscation of Christ's teachings and that required publishing the Bible in the vernacular and removing the mystification of the Church's elaborate rituals.

One of the results of this reform was an arbitrary division between concepts like "religion" and "magic" in the Protestant worldview which became the norm in the West for the next several centuries (up to the late twentieth and early twenty-first century when this dichotomy came to be challenged by a new breed of historians of religion). Roman Catholicism, or "Popery" as it was referred to by Protestants, was tantamount to superstition and magic, a distortion of Christ's original teachings. Religion was pure belief; it was faith in the word of God and in nothing else. Ritual was suspected as being the work of the Devil. By extricating magic from religion, the Reformation had unwittingly pitted all magic against religion. Comfortable—yet purely arbitrary—valuations of "white" or "good" magic versus "black" or "evil" magic became irrelevant. The grace of God descended from On High to the human population below; there was no going in the other direction. There was no possibility of manipulating spiritual forces. Calvinism—the logical conclusion of this sort of fatalism—was the eventual outcome. A human being's destiny was fixed; there was no changing it. The spiritual fate of anyone had been decided long before birth, for God knew everything and therefore had already determined one's destiny.

The reaction against this idea was inevitable. In those pre-Enlightenment days before revolutionary concepts about the rights of human beings became codified, there was a suspicion that human existence was perfectible. There was a belief that life can be improved; that hard work combined with a modicum of luck or divine favor—which can be earned along the way and not predetermined before birth—can result in better circumstances both materially and spiritually. Yet, the prevailing social structures of church and community made it dangerous to express such sentiments openly. The possibility of human perfectibility therefore was something to be pursued in secret, in the study of forbidden books and the practice of forbidden rituals, of magic.

And as human beings can be "perfected," can attain higher spiritual states, so can everything else in creation, and most especially, metals, a belief represented by the equally clandestine practice of alchemy.

Magic can be understood as an expression of the belief that all human experience can be modified, corrected, and improved upon by the deliberate and conscious action of humans themselves. Spiritual power flows in both directions: up and down Jacob's Ladder like the vision of the prophet who saw angels ascending and descending between heaven and earth. Indeed, those very angels themselves could be summoned, could be made to answer the call of the magician, for is it not Christian theology that states that human beings were elevated above the angels by God?

And did not Jesus say to St Peter that what Peter sealed on earth would be sealed in heaven? (Matthew 16:19)

Alchemy and magic thus share a worldview that is somewhat in contradistinction to that of many organized religions. Both the alchemist and the magician are active participants in creation and especially in their own spiritual development. They believe that creation is ongoing, that the natural evolution of metals is towards the perfect metal, gold; that the natural evolution of human beings is towards the perfect human being, the divine Adam. While the activities of the alchemist and the magician are quite dissimilar—the alchemist in the laboratory, the magician in the temple or in a graveyard at night, or in the woods far from human habitation—they both understand that the forces that exist in the world can be manipulated by the wise operator. They do not wait for the Divine Light to descend. They are in a hurry.

In a very real sense, the alchemist and the magician are scientists. The proof of divinity, of spiritual realities, lies in the direct experience of them and is not taken on faith alone. They require tangible proof that their efforts are rewarded, not in the next life but in this one. The magician wants to *see* the angels and the demons with his or her own eyes; the alchemist needs to participate in the physical transformation of metals like lead and iron into gold. In a way, a way that normative religion would reject, the alchemist and the magician are determined to *prove* spiritual reality. Their experiments and rituals are demonstrations of the power of the divine that exists in Creation. They offer tangible evidence of the existence of God and of the veracity of the Scriptures in ways that no average pastor, no seminary-trained minister of Christ, could hope to equal. Yet, for all that, they became outsiders. The alchemist and the magician would never be accepted into the embrace of the church unless they repented of their deeds, unless they destroyed their notebooks and grimoires.

Or unless they went on the offensive, and created their own church.

THE EARLY LIFE OF THE SORCERER

Joseph Smith Jr. was born on December 23, 1805 to Joseph Smith Sr and Lucy Mack Smith in the town of Sharon, Vermont. His parents were familiar with current occult practices at the time, living in the post-Revolutionary War era that was a hotbed of religious experimentation. Joseph Sr. himself was already acquainted with the use of the divining rod for finding buried treasure.

Their fifth child, Joseph Jr., seemed to have been marked at an early age for something important. His birthday was at the winter solstice and nearly on Christmas Eve, the day commonly accepted as the birthday of Jesus. At a young age he developed a bone infection which required his use of crutches for some time. Later, as a pre-pubescent youth with spiritual interests, he began to use the divining rod to find underground sources of water.

His childhood in Vermont took place at a time when there was a tremendous religious revival taking place all over the northern states, from New England to New York and Pennsylvania. The American Revolution, followed by the War of 1812 which began when Joseph Smith Jr was only seven years old, led to tremendous social and economic upheaval in the newly-independent States. His father experienced terrible luck at farming with three years of crop failures in a row and was going bankrupt. He tried to augment his family's meager income with treasure-seeking using a divining rod, but with limited or no success.

A divining rod is normally a forked branch or a specially-made wand of wood or metal that is used to point to the location of buried valuables. The operator holds the forked ends in his/her left and right hand—a bit like a steering wheel—and invokes a higher power to enable him/her to be drawn to the underground location. The rod will then bend towards the spot where the operator should begin digging.

The use of the divining rod was extremely popular throughout that part of the country for more than a hundred years. In fact, the author knew of people using the divining rod in New Hampshire as late as the 1960s, mostly to find water during the drought of 1963–1964.

But finding water or gold was not the only purpose of the divining rod. It could also be used as a means for spiritual communication.

A group known as the Fraternity of Rodmen was active in Vermont at the time the Smiths lived there. The Fraternity was composed of men who—for instance—would use divining rods to determine who built the so-called "Indian burial" mounds by asking if it had been the Egyptians, etc. until the rod would respond at the mention of the Welsh. If the rod did not move, the answer was "no." Any movement was usually interpreted as a "yes." [1]

This went further to the extent that the Fraternity began receiving instructions to build a temple, since they were informed that they were descendants of the Lost Tribes of Israel.

---

1   The idea that the Welsh may have built the mounds was not original with the Rodmen. As august a personality as Dr John Dee—the Elizabethan magician, mathematician and spy—was convinced that the New World had been visited by the Welsh long before Columbus. It was also with Dr. Dee that we have an early example of the use of the "shew stone" or "seer stone" that Joseph Smith used. In Dee's case, the stone was made of obsidian brought over from the New World itself.

The idea that the New World was the ultimate destination of the wandering tribes had tremendous currency in those days, and groups like the New Israelites were formed along the lines of that belief. Other groups insisted that the Native Americans were themselves remnants of the Lost Tribes, while such seventeenth-century luminaries as Cotton Mather claimed that the "Red Men" were in fact Devils incarnate since there was no mention of the Native Americans in the Bible.

Eventually, the group known as the Fraternity of Rodmen began making predictions about the end of the world, which was due to take place—according to their reckoning—on January 14, 1802. One eyewitness to those events remembered hearing that Joseph Smith Sr had been involved with the Rodmen and with their failed prediction concerning the apocalypse of 1802.

This event is mentioned to situate the reader in the place and time in which Joseph Smith Jr had been born and raised. Divining rods, angelic communications, and the all-important seer stones or shew stones—ancestors to the crystal ball—were part and parcel of a religious and spiritual environment that saw the genesis and growth of charismatic religious movements side by side with magic, alchemy and other occult practices.

The Smith family eventually left Vermont for the town of Palmyra, New York about 1816, where Joseph Sr tried to improve his circumstances and where his son Joseph Jr began to work with the occult practices he learned from his father. By 1817 at the earliest Joseph Smith Jr began actively divining for water and by 1819 he was using occult methods to find buried treasure.

It should be noted that this is not an isolated phenomenon. Hard-working people who nonetheless find themselves in straitened circumstances—usually through no fault of their own that they can see—often resort to otherworldly measures through desperation. A farmer with useless land, a drought, or sick cattle may find himself willing to try a divining rod, a seer stone, or more elaborate occult rituals in order to achieve some of the luck that falls on his neighbors. These are people who are perfectly willing to do whatever it takes to succeed in life, but find that they have been thwarted through circumstances over which they have no control. Occultism offers a means to seize that control using unconventional methods. This represents a belief that all events are connected through some invisible medium; that there are hidden forces at work in the world which seem to favor one person rather than another. This may be due to astrological influences—something as simple as being in the right place at the right time—or to something more specific. If astrological influences are at work, then it stands to reason that a close observation of astrological timetables would help ensure the successful outcome of any endeavor. Almanacs were the source for much of this information, and it was understood that planting cycles depended on observance of the lunar calendar, for instance, so why would human cycles of health and wealth not depend on similar planetary positions?

At the same time, the pious were known to pray to God and the saints for help in every stressful circumstance: to heal sickness, or to find a lost article or a missing person, or to protect against an epidemic. Would not that prayer be more efficacious if it was timed to the appropriate astrological cycle?

This mechanistic view of the universe provided a measure of hope to the disenfranchised and dispossessed. After all, the alternative was unthinkable: that some people were simply born lucky while others were destined for a life of misery regardless of their piety, their hard work, or the force of their will. Instead, the universe was like a giant clockwork and all one had to do was get inside the gears and make certain adjustments—through the use of ritual, for the most part—and fortune would smile.

As can be seen, the Smith family was one of many who clung to the belief that divine providence could be manipulated, could actually be *managed*. This was not seen as antithetical to religion but as an extension of religion into mundane reality, a kind of "God helps those who help themselves" way of thinking. It was also a way of taking power back from the priests.

The Protestant Reformation made it possible for average laypersons to conceive of themselves as religious specialists. Until that time, the privilege of representing the Word of God was the province of the priesthood and especially the Catholic Church.

It was, in a sense, a monopoly. Martin Luther changed all of that and made it possible for anyone to read the Bible in the common language and receive revelations directly from God. New churches, new religious movements, denominations and sects sprang up like mushrooms after a spring rain, each with their own prophet and their own revelation. The Reformation offered a kind of democratization of religion, particularly of Christianity, and in so doing made divine contact accessible to everyone. Once the authority of the Catholic Church was denied, then anyone could become a priest, a prophet, a minister of God. This also meant that the old ways of worship could be challenged, and the old canons of the Church altered, changed, amended ... or completely disregarded. Once the Catholic Church ceased to hold a monopoly on Truth and the Law, then anything was (at least potentially) permissible so long as it was presented in the context of Christian culture and Biblical authority.

Magic offered just such an option. Its rituals were couched in Biblical phrases and invocations, with Hebrew and Latin terms and prayers used throughout and thus preserving some continuity with the Old and New Testaments as well as with the institutionalized Church. God was called upon, as was Jesus and various saints as well as the angels and archangels. And just as Roman Catholic priests had the power to cast out demons, so did the new and independent religious specialists.

Such as Joseph Smith.

In 1830, a neighbor—Newell Knight—fell into a fit that was interpreted as demonic possession. It would be Joseph Smith who exorcised the demon in a celebrated case. This was years after he had performed the rites of ceremonial magic in the woods of upstate New York and recovered the fabled golden plates on which was written what would become the Book of Mormon.

THE RITUALS OF THE SORCERER

The Second Book forms a complete treatise on the mysteries of the Cabala and Ceremonial Magic; by the study of which, a man (who can separate himself from material objects, by the mortification of the sensual appetite-abstinence from drunkenness, gluttony, and other bestial passions, and who lives pure and temperate, free from those actions which degenerate a man to a brute) may become a recipient of Divine light and knowledge; by which they may foresee things to come, whether to private families, or kingdoms, or states, empires, battles, victories, &c.; and likewise be capable of doing much good to their fellow-creatures: such as the healing of all disorders, and assisting with the comforts of life the unfortunate and distressed.

—Francis Barrett's *The Magus* (preface)

The occult environment of the early nineteenth century in New England and New York was a mélange of alchemy, divination, and magic. Alchemy was believed to be a source of wealth, so its practice among the poorer population involved frauds, counterfeiters, and hoaxsters. It seemed like a "get rich quick" scheme for many who were suffering because of the economic uncertainty that plagued the early days of the Republic, and they never questioned why it was that these "alchemists" were willing to help them create gold—for a fee, of course—rather than simply make the gold themselves in private. However, there were also serious alchemists in the United States in those days, particularly in Massachusetts and Connecticut where university presidents and professors were involved in a serious study of the subject and often in regular correspondence with like-minded professionals in England and elsewhere abroad.

A key element of the alchemical worldview is the idea of perfection and especially of perfectibility. This is the cornerstone of hermetic thought in general, that human beings are in a process of spiritual evolution which can be "jump-started" through a series of initiations, whether by more highly evolved human beings (such as masters of secret societies) through ritual and training, or via self-initiation through the more solitary practices of alchemy and magic.

Mormonism, in order to be understood, must be viewed through the lens of occultism and particularly of the hermetic form that Joseph Smith embraced throughout his life and especially in the last five years or so when he incorporated Masonic and other ideas—such as differing levels of priesthood—into the Temple. It was as if he had seen something ineffable and had to surround it with a fortress of secrets, passwords, arcane rituals and silence in order to protect it from misuse or profanation.

It can be said that much of the secrecy has gone out of Judaism, Christianity and Islam. The only remaining secrets in these three Abrahamic faiths are to be found in their mystical analogues: in Jewish Kabbalah, Christian mysticism (such as Rosicrucianism), and Islamic mystical sects such as the Sufis. Secrecy and religion do not, as a rule, go together but secrecy and occultism (the very word "occult" means "secret" or "hidden") do. What Smith did was to incorporate a mystical practice or process within a religion, making it the central feature of the organization if not of the faith itself. It is perhaps for this reason more than any other that Mormonism is decried as a "cult."

The basis for this occult approach to religion is to be found in Smith's early spiritual practices. We have mentioned that he began his career by divining for water and for buried treasure. This was not as antinomian as it might appear, since there was a tradition of the divining rod in that part of the world that has continued to the present day. While the alchemist tried to manufacture gold, the diviner simply went looking for it. The diviner's assumption was that the gold already existed—either as ore or as buried treasure—and all that was required was a kind of mystical "ground penetrating radar" to find it. The alchemist's assumption was that all metals naturally evolved towards gold—the perfect metal—and all that was required was to hurry the process along. Since the method for transmuting lead into gold was not written down clearly in a user's manual but had to be discovered by reading Nature itself (as well as the heavily-encoded alchemical manuscripts that were virtually impossible to decipher) the easier approach was to simply look for gold that already existed.

This anyone could do provided they had a forked stick and limitless patience.

But what separated the successful diviner from the failed seeker after gold was the character of the diviner himself (and they were usually men). The diviner had to demonstrate a connection with the invisible forces that guarded the treasure, either through prayer or through some charismatic aspect of his personality. Possession of a divining rod alone was not enough to guarantee success; a certain innate occult power was also required. Thus some diviners were celebrated for their abilities, and this included the young Joseph Smith Jr.

It is generally acknowledged that Smith had a knack for finding things with his divining rod and, later, his "shew stone." It is impossible at this remove to determine the truth of any of these claims or to interpret them within any kind of scientific framework. We can venture a possibility that some of Smith's alleged success with occult methods was due to several factors, most especially Smith's age at the time that these experiments began.

Poltergeist activity, for instance, is believed to occur around teenaged boys and girls, particularly those undergoing some form of emotional or psychological stress. While this phenomenon is by no means scientifically validated to everyone's satisfaction, some recent studies tend to support at least the contention that these events are somehow related to the stress levels of those individuals who suffer from this condition. Knocks, bites, pinching, the levitation of objects, and various other forms of psychokinesis are included in the list of possible poltergeist activity. While the cause-effect relationship is unknown, there is no doubt that poltergeist activity has taken place. The famous Annemarie Schneider case of Rosenheim, Germany in 1967 is just one, well-documented, case that was investigated by physicists from the Max Planck Institute who came away secure in their opinion that no fraud was involved, nor was the poltergeist activity the result of anything they knew of physics. Ms. Schneider—who was nineteen at the time of the investigation— had experienced severe personal trauma prior to the events in question and was believed to have been suffering from neurosis. She was eventually identified as the cause of the poltergeist phenomenon, which took place in the office where she worked as a secretary.

Joseph Smith was growing up in stressful circumstances due to poverty and a set of parents that might be characterized as dysfunctional today, or at least "odd." Contributing to this was the wave of religious fervor combined with occult activity that was sweeping the Burned-Over District of New York at the time of the Second Great Awakening. When Smith began his divining activity in 1817, he was not yet twelve years old. If there is a correlation between psychic phenomena, youth, and emotional stress then Joseph Smith was a prime candidate. Add to that a family that was already involved in various forms of occult activity and you had a laboratory for creating a psychic, a medium, or some other spiritual practitioner. Or someone who pretended to be.

The motivation for seeking perfection may be due to the identification of flaws within one's own personality or circumstances and the desire to erase them or to transform them into something nobler. For a twelve-year-old farm boy with a divining rod, the possibility of becoming something other, something valuable, must have been irresistible. And the pressure to find money, buried treasure, or gold likewise must have been intense. Like a Zen koan, the solution was not necessarily logical.

Making the rounds of bookstores in the early nineteenth century was an encyclopedic work by Francis Barrett, entitled *The Magus*. Published in 1801 in England, it is a compendium of occult lore and most especially of that discipline known as ceremonial magic, taken from such authoritative sources as the *Three Books of Occult Philosophy* by Cornelius Agrippa, as well as the *Fourth Book of Occult Philosophy* (which was attributed, erroneously, to Agrippa, and which has the most direct instructions for the practice of ceremonial magic). While we are not certain precisely when Joseph Smith first set his eyes on this book, it is beyond doubt that he was working with a copy in the period shortly before his death for the design of the talisman he was wearing on the day he was murdered came directly from the pages of *The Magus.*

Ceremonial magic is, as its name implies, a form of magic that relies heavily on the correct performance of ritual. These rituals are designed to contact spiritual forces directly, through the use of invocations, ritual gestures, incenses appropriate to the spiritual force being summoned, etc. The alchemist has his crucible and retort, his alembic and oven. In the alembic, a piece of raw material is sealed and operations performed on it to initiate its physical transformation. The magician, on the other hand, is the raw material of the transformation and the ritual chamber, the magic circle, is his alembic. To simplify, in the alchemist's laboratory lead is transformed into gold. In the magic circle, the lead transforms itself.

Joseph Smith did not understand this at first, not when he was a young teenager practicing magic for the first time. However, as he matured into his role as the Prophet, he realized that the first steps he took on the path of ceremonial magic were leading him towards the same conclusion. This is evident from observing the development of Mormonism from just another quasi-Christian denomination into an initiatory structure with secret ceremonies and higher and higher levels of spiritual responsibility. The end result of all this refinement can only be the apotheosis: the goal of Hermeticism and of ceremonial magic (as well as alchemy) in particular.

The Magus sets all this out quite clearly. While sections of the book are devoted to the manufacture of talismans, "natural magic", alchemy, potions and philtres, and the Kabbalah, the portion of the book that usually attracts the most attention is that on ceremonial magic. Barrett insists that a person be morally pure before engaging in these pursuits, as the quotation that begins this section indicates. Barrett states that the goal of all of this is to attain the Divine Light and to help other human beings in their suffering thereby.

We may find precursors to the Mormon prohibition against alcohol and caffeine in this preface to *The Magus*, but that is purely speculation since many religions have dietary restrictions of various kinds. Purity, however, was an important element of early Mormonism and even of Smith's ability to find the golden plates on which the Book of Mormon was inscribed, as we will see. But the characterization of the magician as someone who is possessed of divinity and uses that power to help others must have impressed itself on the mind of Joseph Smith, who effectively elevated the status of magician to that of divinely-inspired Prophet. The connection between Joseph Smith as magician to Joseph Smith as prophet is a direct one, a solid line rather than a dotted line, for it was the ritual of magic that produced the Book of Mormon and created a religion.

His first operations of ceremonial magic began in earnest on September 22, 1823, one hundred and thirty-one years to the day after the execution of Mary Towne Easty as a witch in Salem, Massachusetts after accusations of witchcraft by Smith's ancestor, Samuel Smith ... an event which the Smith family certainly remembered as Joseph would one day return to Salem to seek buried treasure in his ancestor's neighborhood. It was also the first day of autumn, and the first degree of the sign of Libra. As one of the quarter days of the year (the others being the spring equinox and the winter and summer solstices) it formed part of the occult calendar with which Smith was familiar from his reading of occult texts or from common knowledge as presented in the almanacs of the period.

At the time of this all-important magical operation, Joseph Smith was not yet eighteen years-old.

Up to this time, Smith had been using a "shew stone" or "seer stone." This was a stone that he would put into a hat, and then peer into the hat at the stone and thereby obtain visions. Evidently the placement of the stone in the hat would ensure that Smith could gaze onto the stone in darkness as he held the hat up to his face. This is virtually identical to the practice of gazing into a crystal ball, as no doubt many readers have already surmised.

One of his visions was of a spirit who told him that golden plates were buried in a cave on the Hill Cumorah.

There was no hill named Cumorah at the time, the word "Cumorah" having come from the Book of Mormon itself. There also is some controversy as to just which hill in the Palmyra region would have been Cumorah. The area is riddled with drumlins, which are ripples in the earth caused by glacier movement. None of the drumlins would have had a natural cave, but perhaps that is the point.

In any event, armed with his vision and with instruments necessary for a ritual of ceremonial magic, Smith retired to the hill in question and—at the stroke of midnight on September 22, 1823—performed the occult evocation. It was by his account a success. The golden plates were revealed. However, and according to one version of the story, as he made to grab them from their resting place, an amphibious creature of some sort jumped out of the cave, turned into a man, and hit him on the head, burying the plates once more and keeping them out of the reach of the teenaged magician.

The nature of the creature has been open to some debate, as we will see shortly. That it was amphibious is interesting, for it means a being that can exist in the land and the sea, a potent symbol of the transformative process.

But why did the spirit prevent Smith from taking the golden plates?

According to Smith, it was because Smith's own motives were not pure. He was thinking only of the gold and of enriching himself thereby, and not of higher spiritual matters.

Smith would keep returning to the Hill Cumorah and its mysterious cave year after year, from 1823 to 1827, on the same day. It was in the final ritual of September 22, 1827 that Smith would finally be allowed to take the plates which were covered in a form of hieroglyphics as well as a pair of magic spectacles that would enable him to begin the process of translating what would become the Book of Mormon.

In order to do so, he had to convince the guardian angel of the plates that he was pure of heart and that his motives were blameless.

The angel's name was Moroni.

CHAPTER TWO:

THE ANGEL

Be it known unto all nations, kindreds, tongues, and people, unto whom this work shall come: That Joseph Smith, Jun., the translator of this work, has shown unto us the plates of which hath been spoken, which have the appearance of gold; and as many of the leaves as the said Smith has translated we did handle with our hands; and we also saw the engravings thereon, all of which has the appearance of ancient work, and of curious workmanship. And this we bear record with words of soberness, that the said Smith has shown unto us, for we have seen and hefted, and know of a surety that the said Smith has got the plates of which we have spoken. And we give our names unto the world, to witness unto the world that which we have seen. And we lie not, God bearing witness of it.

The "Testimony of Eight Witnesses" in
The Book of Mormon

THE ANGEL MORONI, who first appeared to Joseph Smith the night before his first operation of ceremonial magic on September 22, 1823, had been a human being before he was an angel. This is an important point, and one which is often neglected or ignored.

Just as Smith grew up in an atmosphere of strange religious sects and occult practices, as well as serious Hermetic work with the goal of human perfection always in mind, so too did some ancient texts imply that humans could become angels and indeed *had* become angels. The most famous of these is the Angel Metatron.

Familiar to students of Jewish mysticism and particularly of *merkavah,* "chariot" or "throne" mysticism, Metatron appears as the name of an angel who sits on a throne in heaven. There are various explanations for Metatron, and there were attempts by early Jewish scholars to link him with Enoch (Gen. 5:24) who was "taken" to heaven by God and presumably transformed from a human being with a corporeal form to something more supernatural.

In the early eighteenth century, a Jewish apocalyptic text was published entitled "The Revelation of Moses," which purported to be a description of how Metatron transformed Moses's body into spiritual substance—i.e., "fire"—in order that Moses may ascend the seven heavens and approach the throne of God. Elijah the prophet of the Old Testament was likewise taken directly—and bodily—to heaven (2 Kings 2:1) where it is presumed he exchanged his corporeal form for something able to withstand the heavenly environment.

Thus, Joseph Smith's Angel Moroni comes from a distinguished line of prophets who were transformed into spiritual entities. These cases especially are interesting because they relate directly to the practice of Jewish mysticism known as "the Descent to the Chariot." This was a process of visualization and ritual in which the mystic ascended the seven heavens to approach the throne of God. The "Chariot" in the title can be taken to mean the chariot that brought the prophet Elijah to heaven as well as the chariot that appeared before Ezekiel, a biblical episode that is directly connected to Ezekiel's vision of a New Jerusalem with a rebuilt Temple of Solomon, a theme that obsessed Joseph Smith in his final years.

Moroni was the son of Mormon, and was entrusted with the golden plates on which the history of his people was written; thus the entire collection of various "books" was published under the name *The Book of Mormon.* Moroni's own genealogy is a key to understanding what the Book of Mormon is all about and the controversies that have bedeviled the text to this day.

Treasure Guardians

Before we look at Moroni specifically, we must first address the most obvious element of the discovery story: that of the amphibian who jumped out of the cave where the treasure was buried. How did the Angel Moroni—who had, after all, once been a human being and a prophet—become transformed into a toad?

In order to answer this question, we have to look at the persistent legends concerning buried treasure and the spirits that guard it.

There was a recurring myth concerning buried treasure in North America, particularly on the eastern seaboard, which was connected with tales of pirates. The basic myth structure has a pirate burying treasure in a remote location and then killing the man who had helped him dig the burial spot, in order that his spirit would continue to guard the treasure. Many of these stories were linked to the romantic legend of the pirate William Kidd (1654-1701), who was eventually captured in Boston and executed in London for piracy. Kidd had buried treasure on Gardiner's Island in New York, but that was retrieved by the governor and used as evidence in the trial against him. Rumors abounded, however, of Kidd having buried treasure all over the world, from Japan and Vietnam to the Caribbean and Canada, and virtually everywhere in between. The treasure remained buried because of Kidd's execution in London in 1701, so treasure hunters began scouring old records or listening to the tall tales of locals in an effort to secure for themselves the hidden gold and jewels.

It is known that Joseph Smith read the stories of Kidd and was enthralled by them (as were many of his contemporaries). The idea that there could be treasure buried anywhere from Nova Scotia to Florida, and from the east coast as far inland as central Pennsylvania, was prevalent not only in fictional literature but as a mainstay of the treasure diviners. (Their modern equivalent might be those who wander along the seashore or the countryside with metal detectors, hoping to find anything from loose change to Spanish doubloons.)

Many of these stories involved the appearance of a ghost who would attempt to frighten the treasure hunters away. The ghost was the spirit of the slain pirate who would often appear as he had when murdered: covered in blood and moaning pitiably. The treasure itself was always in a strong box of some kind, buried in a hole in the ground, and covered with a large stone. One had to lift the stone and then retrieve the box, and do it all without saying a word. Silence was a key issue in the retrieval of this spectral treasure; should the treasure seeker as much as exclaim an "Aha!" the treasure would disappear and all further attempts to find it would be thwarted.

It is interesting to note that the story we have told about Joseph Smith being visited by the Angel Moroni and then finding the buried box, only to have it disappear when Smith's motives were not pure, may not have been the original tale told by Smith.

According to admittedly hostile sources contemporary with Smith, he first told the story of finding the buried box being guarded not by an angel but by the ghost of a murdered man. This man had a long beard and his throat was slit from ear to ear. His clothes were covered in blood. It was the precise image from the treasure-seekers legends with virtually no change of any kind.

According to this version of the story it was only later that it became transformed and with it the murdered pirate became the Angel Moroni who was, of course, first a human being and a prophet and later an Angel.

Mormons contest this reading of course, claiming that the Captain Kidd version was a later interpolation by critics hostile to Mormonism, who wanted to link the otherwise pious Joseph Smith to the mercenary pursuit of treasure-digging and thereby devalue the Book of Mormon and the entire religion upon which it is based.

A long response to the Captain Kidd story by Mormon apologist Larry E. Morris more or less successfully refutes some of these claims but ignores one vital piece of information: that the names of the Hill Cumorah and the Angel Moroni might be linked specifically to Captain Kidd.

One of Kidd's destinations on his piratical tour of the Indian Ocean was the Comoros Islands, which are off the southeastern coast of Africa, near Madagascar. The capital city of the

Comoros is ... Moroni. The suggestion that the Hill Cumorah began as the Comoros to young Joseph Smith, and that the Angel Moroni was christened after its capital city of Moroni, is so compelling that we are forced to consider that maybe the critics have a point. After all, there is no known etymological link between the words Cumorah and Moroni on the one hand and their alleged Jewish origins on the other. The Mormon apologist above-mentioned does not dispute the claim that Joseph Smith was familiar with the Captain Kidd tales, nor does he address the Comoros/Cumorah or Moroni/Moroni coincidence (although others do[2]). Rather, he insists that Smith had a visitation from an Angel on the night of September 21, 1823 and again at the Hill Cumorah on September 22, 1823 and for successive years thereafter, and bases this on Smith's published testimony even though Smith published several versions of this episode which do not completely agree[3], and there is also the version published by his mother, Lucy Mack Smith, which is hagiographic but which does not deny that the family was involved in occult pursuits from time to time.[4]

Mormon apologists usually want to point out that the milieu in which Smith was raised was an amalgam of normative Christian religion with "folk magic" practices, such as the divining rod, and that it would have been unusual for Smith not to have been involved in such practices or to have been aware of them. They insist that the atmosphere of the time was such that the boundary between magic and religion was blurred, at best, or

---

2   Some Mormons object that the Comoros Islands and especially the settlement of Moroni did not appear in atlases or gazettes of the time of Joseph Smith. However, they do not address the likelihood that Smith would have been aware of this geography from stories of William Kidd who did, in fact, visit the Comoros and Moroni during his travels.

3   At times, Smith refers to this Angel as "Nephi" which is one of the prophets in the Book of Mormon.

4   This is also a controversial point, and depends on how one reads the sentence in Lucy Mack's book. Apologists take it to mean that the Smith family never involved itself in magic; critics of Mormonism read the same sentence as meaning they did! There is no consensus of opinion on this issue.

non-existent at worst. They will also cite Biblical precedents, such as Moses and Aaron and their magical battle with the Pharaoh's magicians, for Joseph Smith's activities as a youth.

The author does not dispute any of this. It has been well-documented by responsible academic historians such as John L. Brooke in *The Refiner's Fire* that occult practices flourished alongside normative religion in early nineteenth century America, not only among the farmers and laborers and merchants but also among the educated and the intelligentsia. Religion might have provided solace for the soul, but could do nothing for the soil. Farmers and other workers needed more than piety in order to survive. They needed a mechanism for wresting wealth out of the ground, one way or another. Magic seemed to afford them just such a means and—in the texts known as the grimoires and other magical workbooks—the language was Christian and the approach was sacred. One called upon God and his angels in order to find gold, heal the sick, or locate lost cattle.

That is why this author finds no discrepancy or inconsistency between Smith's alleged treasure-seeking on the one hand and his alleged conversation with an Angel on the other. In the context of ceremonial magic, one calls upon angels (or demons, or spirits of the dead) to find gold, heal the sick, and locate lost cattle. The Captain Kidd interpretation may be more of a distraction than is needed, for the scene of the young sorcerer at midnight on the autumnal equinox conjuring an Angel to find gold is perfectly consistent with the methodology represented in the occult workbooks, such as Francis Barrett's *The Magus*.

Mormon apologists, however, claim that there is no evidence that Smith ever used the entire ritual formula of ceremonial magic that was published in *The Magus* and therefore that Smith did not use the magic circle and other apparatus as listed in *The Magus* to find gold.

This critique has several problems, as anyone who has dabbled in ceremonial magic at all would recognize, so it is perhaps to the credit of the Mormon apologists that they do not have direct experience of this phenomenon and that therefore their reasoning is a little faulty.

Virtually no one in impoverished circumstances would have been able to incorporate all of the elements Barrett (or, actually, the pseudo-Agrippa of the *Fourth Book of Occult Philosophy*) insists are essential to the practice. There are swords, vestments, incenses, parchments, all without number. Special inks made from the blood of specific animals and herbs. Lengthy personal preparations involving sacred baths, etc. Most magicians of the author's acquaintance—and he knows a few—began their occult careers by ignoring most of these requirements and doing the best they could with whatever they had available. So let it be with Joseph Smith. To say that Smith could not have followed the instructions in *The Magus* and therefore did not use the rituals at all implies that all of the other users of *The Magus* did. Smith was seventeen years old at the time of the first September 22 invocation. He would have taken a number of shortcuts.

What would have been possible to do is what it seems he did do: choose a specific time (midnight on the autumnal equinox), go to a secluded location, cast a circle, make an invocation, and wait. It was better than postponing the ritual until all the various implements listed by Barrett could be obtained, consecrated, etc.

Mormons also like to point out that the day chosen—deliberately or accidentally—by Joseph Smith and/or the Angel Moroni for the first conjuration was also the first day of the Jewish New Year, Rosh ha-Shonah. This would have been intriguing, especially in light of the "Descent to the Chariot" idea mentioned above since the Jewish New Year was an important day for this *merkavah* practice, except that September 22, 1823 was *not* Rosh ha-Shonah.

Recourse to Jewish calendars for the year in question demonstrates that September 22, 1823 was not Rosh ha-Shonah but the third day of Sukkoth. Sukkoth is one of the holy days that follow Rosh ha-Shonah and Yom Kippur, both of which took place earlier in September (September 5th and September 14th, respectively). So although this allegation is repeated in many forums, it is incorrect. There was no correlation between the Jewish New Year and the day on which Joseph Smith struggled with an Angel. Thus we are left with the most obvious of all the choices: that September 22 was selected because of its astrological and occult significance as the autumnal equinox.

But what about the toad?

As with everything Mormon, there is controversy over this issue as well. In fact, the reaction of the Mormon hierarchy to a fraudulent document known as the "Salamander Letter" is evidence that the LDS Church did take the toad story as possible fact.

The story briefly is this:

As some contemporaries of Smith record it, Smith told them that when he first went to take the golden plates out of the ground on September 22, 1823, that the treasure was guarded by a toad. The toad then transformed into a larger animal and eventually into a human being or a spirit ... the details are a little hazy and depend on which of the testimonies one reads or believes. In any event, what began as a toad ended as a slap in the head to Joseph Smith and the temporary loss of the plates.

Most historians discount the toad story since it was related either second-hand or third-hand or was published by critics hostile to Mormonism. The issue should have ended there, but in the 1980s a scandal developed in Salt Lake City—at the headquarters of the LDS Church—over the existence of the Salamander Letter.

This forgery pretended to be a letter by one of Joseph Smith's intimates stating that the creature that was guarding the treasure on that first night was a salamander. The head of the LDS Church bought the incriminating document from a man later revealed to have been a master forger—Mark Hofmann—for a huge sum of money, and then promptly buried the document deep in the Mormon vaults where it was determined it should never see the light of day.

Why was the reference to a salamander considered incriminating?

To answer that, we have to return to our treasure-hunting scenario.

One of the features of buried treasure stories is the guardian factor. As we have seen, these can sometimes take the form of men or women who were murdered on-site—usually to protect the secret of the location of the treasure—and whose spirits now haunt the site. Other stories abound in the European literature, especially of demonic guardians of treasure. Such medieval sorcerer's workbooks as the Red Dragon or the Grand Grimoire feature the demon Lucifuge Rofocale, who is in charge of the treasures of the earth. A famous drawing (see below) of this individual shows him to be standing next to a buried pile of gold that is covered by a rock.

As can be seen, this demon appears in a quasi-animal form with a tail, cloven hoofs, and horns which was a typical concept

of the Devil at the time. In European magic, toads, lizards and other amphibians were considered representatives of the Devil or different manifestations of the Devil himself. Buried treasure was their domain, and they had to be propitiated in some way before they would release their bounty. Often, this required a pact. In the popular imagination, this would be an agreement with the Devil, signed in the sorcerer's blood. There are many examples in history of such pacts, and a few actual examples do remain such as the one allegedly signed by Urbain Grandier (of the famous "Devils of Loudon" episode in which the priest, Grandier, was accused of demonolatry in the year 1633 in France).

To make matters more interesting, the popular idea of a salamander was as an elemental figure associated with fire. There was a demonic aspect to the salamander, and if Smith had indeed been confronted with a salamander then the reaction among some Mormons would have been that his entire experience had been the work of the Devil. When Mark Hofmann created his forgery—known as the "Salamander Letter"—he knew what he was doing. He knew that the LDS Church would take any measures necessary to obtain the letter and hide it away forever. The fact that they did so—that they paid a huge sum of money for the letter and then buried it in their vault—is evidence that the Mormons themselves were insecure in their faith and harbored deep suspicions that Smith *was* engaged in occult practices and that the result of those practices was the conjuration of a demon which then gave Smith a bogus scripture.

As it happened, the letter was proven to be a forgery after a series of murders and increasingly desperate steps taken by Hofmann to extort more money from the LDS Church, including a failed bombing attempt which left Hofmann himself injured. The exposure of the affair of the Salamander Letter was an embarrassment for the Church, for it called into question a host of assumptions about Smith, the Book of Mormon, and the Church itself. These assumptions were based on the official doctrine that Smith was not involved in ceremonial magic or occultism. These assumptions would be shown to be faulty at best, or completely erroneous at worst.

It is virtually impossible to separate the circumstances of Joseph Smith's adventure with the golden plates from popular ideas of treasure-digging that were common currency at the time. Mormons insist that there is no connection, or a tenuous connection at best, but historians such as Brooke mentioned above have demonstrated that treasure-digging was a well-known practice and that the steps to be taken were common knowledge in rural New England and New York.

For Smith to have spoken of a buried treasure of golden plates that was protected by a guardian spirit, and of the ritualistic nature of his pursuit of that treasure, can only mean that his story was to be taken in the context of the times. Perhaps Smith's genius lay in elevating the mundane and "superstitious" practice of treasure hunting to something more sublime: in transforming the bloody, murdered pirate or the loathesome toad into an angel in flowing white robes bathed in divine light, and the treasure into a sacred scripture with a new dispensation for humanity. By claiming that the Angel Moroni had once been a human being and was transformed into an angel was consistent with ideas of the ghosts of murdered pirates guarding the buried treasure. And the plates themselves were not clay tablets written in cuneiform or ancient parchments written in Hebrew or Aramaic, but instead were leaves of gold on which was written "Reformed Egyptian." All of the basic elements of the treasure-digging myth had been taken up and subtly but dramatically transformed. Like the Catholic Church's appropriation of the Feast of Saturnalia as Christmas, or the erection of cathedrals on formerly pagan sites, Joseph Smith performed a similar transformation of the occult themes current in his day.

And it worked. After all, a visit to Salt Lake City and the Mormon Tabernacle there would convince anyone that Smith had, indeed, discovered a source of incredible wealth.

CHAPTER THREE

THE NEW RELIGION

... they have also as strong a faith in the power of their ark as ever the Israelites had in theirs, ascribing the success of one party to their stricter adherence to the law, than the other, we have strong reason to conclude them of Hebrew origin. The Indians have an old tradition, that when they left their own native land, they brought with them a *sanctified rod* by order of an oracle, which they fixed every evening in the ground, and were to remove from place to place on the continent towards the sun rising till it budded in one night's time. I have seen other Indians, says the same writer, who related the same thing. Instead of the miraculous direction to which they limit it, in their western banishment, it appears more likely that they refer to the ancient circumstance of the rod of Aaron, which in order to check the murmur of those who conspired against him, was in his favour made to bud blossoms and yield almonds at one and the same time.

> —Mordechai Noah, *Discourse on the Evidences of the American Indians being the Descendants of the Lost Tribes of Israel,* p 13 (emphasis in the original)

IN ADDITION TO THE OCCULT IDEAS popular in early post-Revolutionary America, such as the divining rod and buried treasure, there were alternative histories concerning the new country in which the early Americans found themselves. Like the "ancient astronaut" theories of today, these were based on fragmentary evidence, suggestive associations, suspicion of authority, and energetic speculation. This was a time of obsession about "origins", as the Americans were of European descent (or, in the case of the slaves, African or Native American descent) and had

41

no deep cultural roots in North America. The cities they lived in were the cities they built themselves; there was no admiring of the Renaissance architecture of Italy, or the cafés along the Left Bank in Paris, or shivering at the Tower of London. There were simple homes, simple shops, and few of these were more than a hundred years old by the time Joseph Smith was born.

Thus, the land itself began to take on a mysterious allure. Who lived here before? Were the Native Americans descendants of some other race, some race not mentioned in the Bible? What ghosts haunted the forests of New England and upstate New York? What treasure awaited discovery in the dark and bloody ground? In short: just what had the European settlers and conquerors inherited in this wild and untamed continent?

There were at least two main currents of alternative history at the time. The first involved the archaeological significance of what are commonly referred to as "Indian burial mounds." These structures were found all over the Atlantic seaboard from Florida to New Hampshire and inland as far as Missouri and Texas, and some have survived to this day.

Although referred to as burial mounds, not all of these structures were used for burial. Some had other ritual significance, although details have been lost to time as their builders do not seem to have left any written testimony other than the odd petroglyph of uncertain provenance. Some of the mounds clearly had an astronomical purpose (like Stonehenge in England) and were of staggering size and complexity. We can mention the famous Serpent Mound in Adams County, Ohio as only one of these, a fabulous structure dated anywhere from 250 to 1000 CE. Other mounds, at Marietta and Chilicothe, Ohio and at Moundsville, West Virginia, are mute testimony to the labors of a fantastic race of pre-Columbians that thrived more than a thousand years before modern Europeans began arriving.

Some digging in these mounds often resulted in the discovery of pottery, ancient jewelry, or other artifacts—including curiously carved stone tablets—thus fueling a cottage industry in amateur archaeology and treasure-hunting. Even Cotton Mather—an observer at the Salem witchcraft trials—was aware of the strange stone carvings and mentioned them in his *Magnalia Christi Americana* published in 1702. However, the nature of the builders themselves had not been determined conclusively thereby allowing for all forms of imaginative theories some of which have persisted till the present time in the continued absence of definitive identification.

This led to the second main current of speculative history, which was that of the Lost Tribes of Israel.

The idea that ten of the original twelve tribes of Israel were "lost" has been persistent through the thousands of years that have passed since the Babylonian Exile. Today, there is considerable controversy over this issue and even if any of the tribes could be considered to have been truly "lost" at all, and not merely assimilated into local cultures. Prior to the late twentieth century, however, the idea that ten of the twelve tribes were lost and scattered throughout the world proved to be seductive. Many theories were put forward, including the idea that descendants of the lost tribes included western Europeans, certain African groups, the Irish, the British, etc.

One of the most prevalent theories was that the Native American population was descended from the Jews. This idea probably began with the voyages of a seventeenth century Portuguese explorer, Antonio de Montezinos, who claimed he had found Jewish descendants among the Native Americans of what is now Ecuador. He was actually able to convince a noted Dutch Rabbi—Menasseh ben Israel—of this theory, and ben Israel published an account of this in *The Hope of Israel*, a book printed in London in 1650. The impact of this book was tremendous, and the theory was repeated in various forms and among various groups around the world.

One of the proponents of this theory in the United States was a president of the Continental Congress and director of the US Mint, Elias Boudinot (1740–1821). Boudinot was an important early supporter of citizenship for Black Americans as well as the Native American population; it is possible that his beliefs concerning the Jewish origins of the Native Americans helped fuel his position.

Another prominent American who subscribed to the Native American theory was Mordechai Noah (1785–1851). Noah, a Jewish-American and a Freemason, who was named US consul to Tunis at the time of the Barbary Coast piracy episode, wrote a forty-page pamphlet detailing the evidence for the Jewish origins of the Native American tribes. His *Discourse on the Evidences of the American Indians being the Descendants of the Lost Tribes of Israel* was published in 1837, seven years after the first publication of the Book of Mormon in 1830, which indicates how strong this belief had survived the nearly two hundred years since the publication of Rabbi ben Israel's book in London. It further illustrates the popularity of this idea at the time Joseph Smith "translated" his epic work into English, which gave the Native American theory the force of scripture. Mordechai Noah was a well-known journalist and politician at the time Joseph Smith was involved in treasure-digging in western New York and, indeed, at least one of Noah's articles on the Jewish origin of the Native Americans was published in Smith's local newspaper, the *Wayne Sentinel,* on October 11, 1825 and thus right in the middle of the Moroni conjurations (1823–1827) and five years *before* the Book of Mormon was published.

According to the Book of Mormon, one of the lost tribes— that of Joseph, through the tribe of Manasseh—made it to North America six centuries before the birth of Jesus. This is a critical issue in the entire Mormon worldview. A corollary to this is the revelation that Jesus himself appeared in North America after his resurrection (3 Nephi 11—36).

The tale begins with the story of Lehi, a member of the lost tribe of Joseph, who flees Jerusalem before its sack by the Babylonians in the sixth century BCE. He and his family travel by ship to America. From that time until about 130 BCE, the story is largely about Lehi and his descendants. By 130 BCE, however, the descendants of Lehi split into two opposing forces, the Nephites and the Lamanites.

However, the descendants of Lehi were not the first inhabitants of the American continent. According to the Mormon Book of Ether, a group called the Jaredites had come to the western hemisphere around the time of the Tower of Babel, almost two thousand years before the arrival of the Lehi family.

Recent archaeological and biological/genetic research and testing has shown that there is no scientific evidence for a Near Eastern or Middle Eastern origin of the Native American population. The emphasis is still on an Asian—and specifically Mongolian or Siberian—origin. In light of this, the newest Introduction to the Book of Mormon tends to qualify its position concerning the Native Americans and Jewish ancestry. However, this might be missing the point.

While scientific breakthroughs in DNA testing—and corresponding archaeological breakthroughs in the dating of America's earliest humans—mitigate against Mormon claims of Jewish ancestry for the Native Americans, there is another option to consider.

Prompted by anomalous discoveries in ancient Native American mounds, several researchers began to come up with linguistic and other evidence to show that the North American continent (at least) had been visited by groups from across the Atlantic Ocean long before the arrival of Christopher Columbus in 1492. Barry Fell, a marine biologist at Harvard University, published several books that purported to show that North America had been visited by members of civilizations from Europe and North Africa. He based this theory on his translations of petroglyphs (inscriptions carved into rocks) found all over the continent. While Fell's theories have been dismissed by mainstream academics on the basis of what they claim is faulty methodology, recently there has been grudging acknowledgement[5] that Fell did, indeed, discover ancient Celtic ogham runes on North American rocks. This indicates that the petroglyphs may be as old as the first century BCE or as late as the fifth or sixth century CE (the widest possible range being allowed, as the precise dating of ogham is fraught with controversy). Ogham was used as a script by the ancient Celts, so to find it carved into rocks in

---

5 Most notably by Canadian archaeologist David H. Kelley in an important 1990 article about Fell, published in the *Review of Archaeology*.

North America is suggestive indeed of ancient travelers predating Columbus by at least one thousand years.

Other ancient carvings found in North America have less to do with the Celts and more to do with a possible Middle Eastern origin.

Let us consider the Bat Creek stone which was discovered in a burial mound in eastern Tennessee in 1889. It bore carvings that were eventually identified in 1971 (almost one hundred years after its discovery and therefore not the product of fraud) as ancient Hebrew. In fact, it was a type of Hebrew used in the first century CE and is believed to translate as "For Judea". In 1988, the site was carbon-dated to a range of years from 32 CE–769 CE. That means that the latest the stone could have been carved is more than seven hundred years *before* Columbus. While the stone is the subject of serious academic controversy, there seems to be no doubt at this time that the stone was carved in first century Hebrew and that the site is as old as it has been claimed. There is simply no explanation for its presence buried in Tennessee soil in 1889.

In New Mexico, we discover the Los Lunas stone. This stone boulder (claimed to have been first discovered in the 1880s by a local farm boy) was covered in Hebrew writing as well, but in a form of Hebrew—sometimes called Paleo-Hebrew—that was used during the time of the first Temple. In other words, it would have been inscribed around the time Joseph Smith's Book of Mormon claimed that Lehi had fled Israel. Indeed, this inscription was not translated until 1949 when it was interpreted to be an abbreviated form of the Ten Commandments. Naturally, this provenance is not accepted by most scholars, who feel that the lack of any other evidence of Jewish habitation at the site renders the discovery suspicious at best.

It is not my intention to get involved in a serious discussion of epigraphy, petroglyphs, or the fact or fiction of early Jewish settlements to the New World. What is important to realize is the impact that these theories had on society in general at the time Joseph Smith was alive and before he wrote the Book of Mormon. We know for instance that George Washington was interested in the burial mounds and that Thomas Jefferson began his own a scientific excavation of a mound in 1781. Jefferson's Secretary of the Treasury, Albert Gallatin, was certain of the value to history of the mounds. Even President of the United States William Henry Harrison would publish his own study of the mounds in 1838 with his *Discourse on the Aborigines of the Valley of the Ohio.*

Thus, it may be relevant to suggest that Joseph Smith's "Lost Tribes" were not the progenitors of the Native American population as Smith's view insists, but that they could have conceivably lived side by side with the local populations until they died out on their own. That there is evidence of a Jewish presence in North America prior to the Columbus arrival is, if not proven to everyone's satisfaction, still a serious historical possibility and cannot be dismissed.

These two themes—burial mounds and ancient Jews in America—are central to the Mormon thesis. Without them, there would be no Book of Mormon at all. And, as we have seen, these two themes are intimately related for the discovery of Jewish inscriptions in burial mounds suggests that the Joseph Smith story had its origins in popular ideas concerning the very nature of America itself, ideas that were in heavy circulation in the early nineteenth century and had little to do with lofty ideas about democracy and the Rights of Man.

IDEOLOGIES

CHAPTER FOUR

THE BOOK OF MORMON

Yea, I make a record in the language of my father, which
consists of the learning of the Jews and the language of the
Egyptians. And I know that the record which I make is true;
and I make it with mine own hand; and I make it according
to my knowledge.

—*Nephi 1:2–3*

JOSEPH SMITH HIMSELF STATES that his vision of September 21,
1823 included the reference to the burial spot of a text "... written upon gold plates, giving an account of the former inhabitants of this continent ... and that the fulness of the everlasting
Gospel was contained in it ... ".

We can see that Smith was careful to say that the account
was of the *former* inhabitants of the North American continent,
not the current ones (i.e., the Native Americans). It would have
been an interesting curiosity had the text remained merely an
imaginative version of who may have lived in America before the
Native Americans arrived. However, it was the next line that cata-
pulted what would become the Book of Mormon into eternal
controversy, for "the fulness of the everlasting Gospel" became
an essential component of this story of burial mounds and the
Jewish tribes cavorting and praying and murdering among
them. Somehow, Smith had connected current popular ideas
about the mounds and about the Lost Tribes to a new Gospel
and thus to a new religion.

What, then, is the Book of Mormon? How did it come to be?

When Joseph Smith was finally allowed to take the golden
plates on September 22, 1827 after four years of trying, he had
an artifact that was written in strange hieroglyphics as well as a
pair of magic spectacles that would allow him to read the hiero-

glyphics and interpret them. The nature of the spectacles is also, as with everything Mormon, controversial.

Some say that they were an actual pair of glasses made of different colored lenses. Others that they were not spectacles at all, but a pair of stones—the Urim and Thummim—with which Smith performed the translation. Others that the stone or stones were placed into Smith's hat—just like the shew stones he was used to using—and that he saw the translations in the crystal vision.

Whatever version is correct, the ultimate take-away from this is that Smith did not actually write down the translation of the Book of Mormon himself. He dictated it to a string of scribes.

The first such scribe was a local Palmyra farmer named Martin Harris. Martin Harris was not only well-to-do, he was also well-disposed towards Smith. As someone who changed his religion constantly, Harris saw in Smith a spiritual prodigy. He would later be one of the all-important Three Witnesses who testified that they had seen the gold plates of the Book of Mormon with their own eyes. (However, Harris would later recant his testimony.)

From roughly December of 1827 to June of 1828, Harris took down 116 pages of text. At one point, Smith had copied some of the mysterious hieroglyphics in which the golden plates were written, and Harris took this paper with him to New York in order to verify the authenticity of the Book of Mormon. He visited a professor of classical linguistics at Columbia College (later to become Columbia University)—one Charles Anthon—who, Harris claimed, acknowledged the authenticity of the hieroglyphics and the translation given by Smith. This account of the meeting was disputed, including by Anthon himself, who declared in subsequent interviews that he believed the document to be a hoax and Martin Harris to be either deluded or insane. A copy of this piece of paper bearing the "Reformed Egyptian" hieroglyphics was among the forgeries sold as genuine by Mark Hofmann to the LDS Church in 1980.

Satisfied that the Book of Mormon was genuine and that Smith was not deceiving him, Harris continued work as a scribe for the Prophet. After having copied down Smith's dictation in the amount of 116 pages, Harris begged to be allowed to show the manuscript to his wife and neighbors. Smith reluctantly agreed. The manuscript was then promptly stolen by either Harris's wife—who disapproved strongly of Smith and probably of

The "Reformed Egyptian" Anthon Transcript as made available through the Community of Christ Church, said to be the original seen by Anthon and possessed by one of the Three Witnesses, David Whitmer.

There is controversy over this identification as well. Anthon said that the figures had been drawn in columns and that there had been the drawing of a crude Aztec calendar on the paper he saw. The Hofmann forgery solved this problem.

her somewhat erratic husband in general—or some friends of his wife, and was never seen again. Its current condition and whereabouts are unknown.

After this debacle, the Angel Moroni became understandably upset with his prophet and took the plates and their accompanying "interpreters" (i.e., the spectacles or stones) away and did not give them back to Smith until September 22, 1828. (Notice the recurrence of the September 22 date in this story.)

Smith then fled from his upstate New York home to the town of Harmony, Pennsylvania in order to work on the translation, citing bizarre circumstances that were conspiring to keep him from working with the text. We do not know exactly what these circumstances were, but they were evidently caused by evil supernatural agencies that did not want the Book of Mormon to be translated.

Not much was accomplished in the translation process until the arrival of Oliver Cowdery at the Harmony farm in April of 1829. At that point, work began apace and by June 1, 1829 most of the Book of Mormon had been translated, with the balance completed by July 1, 1829. Printing of the book—financed by Martin Harris, who basically mortgaged his farm to do it—began in August of that year and was not completed until March 1830.

Part of the reason for the long leadtime between August 1829 and March 1830 lay in the extreme measures that were taken to protect the manuscript. It had to be brought by hand to the printing office—accompanied by guards—and then returned to Smith every evening. After the loss of the first 116 pages in Palmyra in 1828, Smith was taking no chances.

The rumors had begun to fly even before the book was printed, however. The stories were all about how Smith found a "golden bible" buried in the earth, and of course everyone wanted to know what was in it. Many thought Smith was just a conman and a crook. As the episode was revealed that Harris had copied 116 pages that then disappeared, causing Smith to begin—not with the text of those missing pages but—at a different place in the encrypted text thus ignoring the pages already translated, it seemed that the fix was in. Smith could not start at the beginning with the missing pages since he would never have been able to remember what he had dictated. He had to start somewhere else, otherwise the hoax—if it was a hoax—would have been revealed when and if the missing pages ever were discovered.

OUTLINE OF THE BOOK OF MORMON

The Book of Mormon is actually one of many "books" that comprise the entire manuscript, but the aggregate is referred to as the Book of Mormon since it was compiled by the prophet Mormon.

Briefly, the breakdown is as follows:

The first six books comprise the "Small Plates of Nephi." Nephi was the son of Lehi, the first of the Jews who came to America at the time of the destruction of the first Temple. That means that the Book of Mormon begins at roughly 600 BCE. These six books are named as follows, with dates corresponding to the events related as per the official LDS chronology:

1 Nephi	circa 600 BCE
2 Nephi	588–545 BCE
Jacob	544–421 BCE
Enos	420 BCE
Jarom	399–366 BCE
Omni	323–130 BCE

This section is followed by the short Words of Mormon, dated to about 385 CE when the prophet and warrior Mormon gives his son, Moroni, the plates on which are recorded the entire Book of Mormon save the last two sections which are written or translated by Moroni himself.

Thus, Mormon's abridgement and commentary on the Large Plates of Nephi run from Mosiah to chapter seven of Mormon. As follows:

Mosiah	130–91 BCE
Alma	91–52 BCE
Helaman	52–1 BCE
3 Nephi	1 CE–35 CE
4 Nephi	35–321 CE
Mormon	321–421 CE
Ether	(concerns the Jaredites, who were in America two thousand years before Lehi and his family arrived)
Moroni	401–421 CE

Mormon's abridgement of the Large Plates ends, as mentioned, with chapter seven of Mormon. From chapter eight to the end of Mormon is the work of Moroni who also added the sections entitled Ether and Moroni.

In 421 CE, according to the chronology offered by the LDS Church, Moroni—the last of the Nephite prophets—sealed the record and buried it, to be discovered later by the foretold Joseph Smith.

A few important events can be discovered through close reading of the entire Book of Mormon. As early as 1 Nephi chapter 13 we read that America is seen in a vision. By chapter 18, Lehi and his family of Jewish refugees—including his son Nephi and his brothers and sisters—arrive in America. This would be around 591 to 589 BCE. Thus, from the very beginning, the Book of Mormon is an American scripture with an American focus. As the language in several other sections reveals, America is considered equivalent to the Promised Land.

In 2 Nephi chapter 4, Lehi dies. This takes place about 588–570 BCE according to the LDS chronology. After this event, the Nephites and the Lamanites (a tribe descended from the brothers of Nephi, "cursed" by dark skin whereas the Nephites are white) separate from each other, forming two distinct tribes. They never really get along after that. In fact, the Lamanites will eventually destroy the Nephites entirely at a battle that will take place at the Hill Cumorah.

In Jacob, chapter 10, God tells the Nephites that no king will rule in America, that it will be a land of freedom. In verse 19 of chapter 10, God says "I will consecrate this land unto thy seed, forever, for the land of their inheritance." Compare this to the promise God gave to the original Jacob in Genesis 28:13: "There above it stood the Lord, and he said, I am the Lord, the God of your father Abraham and the God of Isaac. I will give you and your descendants the land on which you are lying." This reiterated the original promise of God to Abraham himself in Genesis 15:18–21.

Clearly, then, America was seen as a Promised Land in the Book of Mormon. But ... promised to whom? If we take the first few books literally: a Lost Tribe of Jews descended from the Tribe of Joseph. That would seem to be unusually exclusionary, even for Mormons. But there was a safety clause: since the Nephites would eventually accept Jesus as their Lord, then the Gentiles who did likewise were also accepted into the New World's version of the Promised Land.

This is not so strange as it first appears, for in the nineteenth century there was a movement to offer land in America to the Jews as a sanctuary. In general, America was considered already a sanctuary; but in 1825 and thus around the time that Joseph Smith was conjuring angels in upstate New York the Jewish diplomat and journalist Mordechai Noah was attempting to establish a Jewish refuge on Grand Island in the Niagara River, in Erie County, New York, to be called Ararat (after the mountain where Noah's ark rested after the Flood).

Since this event—which flopped miserably—was very much in the news in 1825 and thus two years before Smith actually obtained the golden plates, it is possible that this story made it into the Smith scripture or at least influenced the entire project. And in actuality the date for the establishment of Ararat was in September: the same month in which Smith would meet the Angel Moroni every year.

Noah was also a believer at one time in the Jewish origin of the Native Americans, something of which the young Smith would have been aware. In fact, there are so many connections between Mordechai Noah's career and beliefs and those of the Mormons that it is difficult to separate them, or to account for these similarities as mere coincidences.

In the book of Mosiah, we come across mention of the seer stones. In chapter 28, Mosiah uses the two seer stones the same way Smith would use them: to translate plates on which were written—in this case—the Jaredite story.

Smith himself describes his seer stones as the Urim and Thummim, a clear reference to the Biblical device that was used for divination by the high priest of the Jews before the destruction of the First Temple. Scholars are divided as to the physical nature of the Urim and Thummim, and even what the Hebrew words mean. While it seems certain from the way they are portrayed (for instance, in 1 Samuel 14:41) that they were used for divination similar to the way we would flip a coin today, there was never any indication that they could be used to "translate" a document. They seem to have been used for purely binary "yes" or "no" type questions. In Smith's case, however, they were referred to as "interpreters" and "seer stones" and even as "spectacles," which gives some idea as to how they would have been used by him. If we remember our crystal ball allegory, we can imagine that Smith would gaze either into or through the two seer stones and thereby "read" the decrypted text, dictating the results to Martin Harris or Oliver Cowdery. It is only in the Book of Mormon that we have the strange juxtaposition of a set of golden plates and a pair of magic spectacles to read them, a construct that appears in Mosiah and then again in Smith's own life.

Shortly after Mosiah uses the two seer stones, however, war breaks out between the Nephites and the Lamanites, as detailed in the book of Alma. This conflict continues for some time, the only respite being in 3 Nephi when—in chapter 11—Christ appears in North America.

This is said to occur shortly after the resurrection, and the events of the book of 3 Nephi are dated by the LDS Church as having taken place from 1 to 35 CE. If we accept the traditional date of Christ's crucifixion as 33 CE then he appeared to the Nephites less than 2 years after his death.

The Book of Mormon contains many references to Jesus long before his appearance in America. His birth is predicted, as well as his death at the hands of his enemies. Jesus occupies a central role in Mormon theology, even though he may not be the Jesus that a Christian would immediately recognize. In 3 Nephi, Jesus informs his followers that Israel will build a New Jerusalem in America, and that the Lost Tribes would be gathered up there. In America, not in Israel.

This is a key factor in contemporary Mormon thinking, and is what lies behind the famous Mormon genealogical obsession. To the Mormons, the Native American population of today is largely descended from the Lamanites. If the Lamanites are descendants of the Tribe of Joseph (the Biblical tribes of Manasseh and Ephraim), then in order for all of the Lost Tribes to come together, the Native Americans must be incorporated into the gathering. But what of the other tribes?

Mormons hope that by genealogical research—and now especially genetic testing as well—they would be able to identify members of the other Lost Tribes. The genealogical research—known in Mormon parlance as "temple work"—first begins with individual Mormons who trace their ancestry back as far as possible. They want to be able to convert their ancestors to Mormonism since they presumably never had a chance to do so while they lived. This "baptism of the dead" as it is sometimes called is one result of the research.

Another result is the drive to determine whether or not any of the Native American population could be descended from the Lamanites or the Jewish people generally. With the advent of DNA analysis, the general consensus among scientists is that today's Native Americans are descended from Asian peoples originating around the Altai mountain range where Mongolia and China meet Russia and Kazakhstan, the nearest Chinese city being Urumqi. No markers were found indicating Jewish or Middle Eastern origins in Native American DNA, so this should have put the controversy to rest. However, it did not.

Mormon geneticists and apologists put forward many arguments for this lack of evidentiary proof of Lamanite origins for the American Indians. In some cases it was suggested that the gene pool had been diluted over the centuries, an explanation that is unscientific considering the persistence of DNA markers over hundreds of thousands of years. Other explanations given include the theory that the Lamanites were only a small community in North America and that the Native Americans came later and overwhelmed the tiny population, or that the Lamanites included the Native Americans in their population through conversion or conquest; but that did not match the accounts given in the Book of Mormon for the existence of millions of Jews on the continent as late as the fifth century CE. It also does not match the official LDS Introduction to the Book of Mormon that still insists that the Native Americans are descendants of the Lamanites.

There is also the conceit that the Lamanites were "cursed" with dark skin (2 Nephi 5:21: "... the Lord God did cause a skin of blackness to come upon them. And thus saith the Lord God; I will cause that they shall be loathsome unto thy people ..."). As the enemy of the more pious (and considerably whiter) Nephites, the implication is clear: black skin equals evil. Thus it was not until 1978 that African Americans were permitted to become Mormon priests and to become involved in the temple ceremonies, although there were Black members of the LDS Church as early as Smith's own lifetime and Smith himself was known to support the abolitionist movement when he was running as a candidate for president. But race is obviously a genetic factor, and thus the Mormon approach to geneaology becomes a complicated brew of race, ethnicity, spiritual approval, ancient origins, Lost Tribes, politics, and the baptism of the dead. As one can see, in Mormonism we have many of the features of the modern New Age and alternative or speculative history phenomenon.

And in fact it becomes a little more "New-Agey" by the time we get to 3 Nephi 28. When Jesus came to America he appointed Twelve Disciples. Of the Twelve, three became immortal. These three Nephites—according to the Book of Mormon—live among us today and are the topic of much Mormon folklore. We may find echoes of this idea in the figures of such Biblical personalities as Enoch and Elijah—who became immortal and who, in the case of Elijah, may still walk among us—or the fabled Nine Unknown Men of Talbot Mundy's novel (1923). This also finds reverberations in Theosophy's Great White Brotherhood and Madame Blavatsky's Mahatmas: advanced beings or "ascended masters" who walk among us unrecognized.

Those three Nephites were the lucky ones. By chapter 6 of the book entitled Mormon, there was a big battle at the site of Hill Cumorah. By chapter 8, the Lamanites had destroyed the Nephites, and Mormon himself was dead. This took place in the fifth century CE. Thus, in 421 CE, Moroni—who had written chapter 8 and the remaining sections of the Book of Mormon—was entrusted with hiding the golden plates that were the record of the Nephites and their centuries-long struggle in North America. They would not be seen again for 1400 years.

The themes that will occupy Mormon thought for the next 180 years are found everywhere in the Book of Mormon. The origins of the Native Americans. America as the Promised Land. The gathering of the Lost Tribes. Seer stones and golden plates. Racial struggles. And all within a Christian framework.

Critics point out that the language—and some of the text—of the Book of Mormon is lifted from the King James Version of the Bible, a book with which Joseph Smith was certainly familiar. The rest of the Book of Mormon is more problematic, of course. With its basic theme of America as the site of the New Jerusalem and the appearance of Jesus among Jewish tribes in America in the first century, CE we have what can be considered a rather brilliant amalgamation and expansion of the ideas and speculations that fueled the imaginations of Americans at that time. Add to that the fact that the golden plates were discovered via acts of ceremonial magic and conjuration, with special attention paid to the astrological calendar, and translated with the equivalent of a crystal ball, and you have not a scripture, perhaps, but a compelling fantasy novel.

Thus the Book of Mormon is very much a product of its time and place and is not as anomalous as many Mormons would believe. But does that make it a hoax?

For purposes of comparison, how did Moses get the Law transcribed onto those stone tablets?

Twice?

Mormonism may give us the key to understanding religion in a different way. Atheists have always complained that religion itself is a hoax, a collection of fairy tales for the intellectually-challenged. Marxists generally agree: religion is the opiate of the people, a technique to keep the masses distracted from their exploitation by the rich who mouth religious platitudes they don't believe in order to keep control over those who do.

To an extent, both of these points of view are correct. Religion has been used to manipulate and control the credulous. It's part of the arsenal of psychological warfare. Appeals to an invisible but higher power will always work on large segments of the population that seek an easy answer to life's uncertainties and a strong leader who talks directly to God. The magicians and alchemists of the world—people like Joseph Smith, in fact—take it upon themselves to by-pass organized religion (to eliminate the middle-man, so to speak) in order to gain direct experience of the divine. Sometimes they are lucky, and get a nod in their direction by some weird, inexplicable event or dramatic change of circumstances. Sometimes they are not so lucky and, like the spirit medium who has to fake every séance even though the first one was real, they find themselves forced to ever grander claims of spiritual contact in order to validate the first one.

It is too easy to call Joseph Smith a swindler and a fraud. He may have been all of those things, but something happened to the uneducated, barely-literate barefoot farmboy from Sharon, Vermont in the autumn of 1823. Something dramatic, something that actually did change the world (or a part of it). Maybe not for the better, maybe not for the worse, but change it *it did.*

Compared to Moses, Smith was a superstar. Moses had the education and the training—among the priests and magicians of ancient Egypt—to create a religion out of the odds and ends of the Egyptian, Babylonian and other pagan elements that were common in his day, and was helped along the way by various scribes who cobbled together what became the Torah over a period of centuries. Smith had no such advantages. His "Torah" flew fully-formed out of his mouth. Complete. In one go.

The stories of the angels, and the seer stones, and the golden plates just might have been a kind of gypsy fortune-teller window-dressing to dazzle the rubes. The golden plates are gone, you say? So are the Tablets of the Law. So is the Ark of the Covenant. What's your point?

Is the strength of Judaism and the entire Judaeo-Christian-Islamic tradition based on the stories of miracles and madmen, or is it to be found in the spiritual and moral teachings of their respective scriptures? From the vision of one human being alone in a desert, or a cave, or a forest in upstate New York, we have the Torah, the Qur'an, the Book of Mormon.

So maybe the Indians are not descended from a weird Jewish tribe called the Lamanites. Maybe Jesus didn't visit America after he rose from the dead in Palestine. I submit that the author of the Book of Mormon just might have been one of America's greatest storytellers, a novelist along the line of a Melville, minus the humor.

And then everything got out of hand.

CHAPTER FIVE

PIETY'S RAINBOW:
THE FATAL TRAJECTORY
OF JOSEPH SMITH, PROPHET

The "Book of Mormon" has been placed in our hands. A viler imposition was never practised. It is an evidence of fraud, blasphemy and credulity, shocking to the Christian and moralist. The "author and proprietor" is one "Joseph Smith, jr." —a fellow who, by some hocus pocus, acquired such an influence over a farmer of Wayne county, that the latter mortgaged his farm for $3,000, which he paid for printing and binding 5000 copies of this blasphemous work.

—*The Geneva Gazette,* April 28, 1830

THE BOOK OF MORMON WAS PUBLISHED in March of 1830, when Smith was not yet 25 years old. Martin Harris had paid for its publication through the mortgaging of his farm in Palmyra, New York.

It was not a best-seller.

It is interesting to conjecture at this remove whether or not Smith initially intended the book to be a new scripture when he was first dictating its pages. After all, there were many predecessors to the Book of Mormon when it came to using Biblical sources as inspiration for the view that America was the Promised Land and the Native Americans were Jewish descendants, as we shall see. One of the most prominent of these was first published in 1823 and then again in 1825: just when Smith was in the midst of his occult activity on Hill Cumorah and at the same time that Mordechai Noah was writing on the same theme. This was *View of the Hebrews or The Tribes of Israel in America,* by Ethan Smith (no relation to Joseph Smith). As one can see from the title alone, virtually all of Smith's major historical themes are covered by Ethan Smith's book, published seven years before the Book of Mormon.

But Ethan Smith's book was not a scripture. It was written in the style of English common at the time and made no pretenses toward a "King James" vernacular, which is how most of the Book of Mormon is written. One of the standard complaints against the Book of Mormon is precisely that its style of English is virtually identical to that of the King James Bible. Why would Joseph Smith, who was translating the golden plates directly from "Reformed Egyptian" into English, not use the style of English common at the time, the style he actually spoke? It is as if it had to be translated first into contemporary nineteenth century American English and then from there back into seventeenth century King James English: a double translation. The only reason for this bizarre decision had to be that he wanted the Book of Mormon to resemble the most famous scripture of his time and place. In order for it to be accepted as a scripture, it had to sound like the only scripture anyone knew.

Critics condemned the book with dozens of similar observations and mostly with ridicule, and the attacks began even before the book was published. As early as June of 1829, a local area newspaper printed the title page, which itself aroused hostility: *The Book of Mormon: an account written by the hand of Mormon, upon plates taken from the Plates of Nephi.* Smith had taken the title page to the federal district court in order to secure his copyright, and at the same time tried to interest local publishers in printing the book. One of these, E.B. Grandin, printed the title page in his *Wayne Sentinel* as a "curiosity." The immediate response of the public seemed to be that the book was a combination of "imposition" and "superstition."

It would cost $3000 to print and bind 5000 copies of the book in 1830. Smith did not have the money, and prevailed upon his friend Martin Harris to use his house as collateral to raise at least half of the cash. In the end, because Smith was unsuccessful in finding anyone else who would underwrite the publication, Harris would wind up fronting the entire amount and losing his home as a result. Although Harris never complained about this to the press, the press nevertheless considered him a dupe of Smith. But this was not the end of the controversy.

Newspapers all over the area began reporting the existence of the "Golden Bible" long before and long after its publication. It was generally treated as a news item of some curiosity at best, or as a scandal at worst. Even such a notable journalist as Mordechai Noah himself would get involved in the furor, on the anti-Mormon side. It is possible that Noah's involvement disturbed Smith, since Noah would have seemed to him to be a logical ally.

One can immediately ascertain the positive or negative view of Smith taken by correspondents by the way they printed his name. If the view was neutral or favorable, he was called "Joseph Smith" or "Joseph Smith, jr.". If the report was unfavorable, he was invariably called "Jo" or "Joe" Smith. The use of the diminutive form of Joseph implied a devaluing of the overall message. How could anyone take seriously a self-appointed prophet with the name "Joe Smith"?

And prophet he was, at least to his small circle of followers. He began to ordain priests in his new religion in 1829, even before the Book of Mormon was published. This was coming at a time when a proliferation of new religions was in the news everywhere in the northern part of the United States. Strange sects with charismatic leaders were popping up in Vermont, northern New York, and elsewhere making it difficult for another group to distinguish itself as different from all the rest.

For instance, as early as 1796 the "Prince and Prophet" Richard Brothers, of Canada, had published "A Revealed Knowledge of the Prophecies and Times. Book the First. Written under the Direction of the LORD GOD" which concerned, among other things, "the restoration of the Hebrews to Jerusalem by the Year 1798," advertised in the *Albany Register* of June 10, 1796. When the restoration did not take place, the wind rather went out of Brothers' sails.

About twenty years later, on October 13, 1817, the *Albany Daily Advertiser* would report the existence of the Vermont Pilgrims. Led by Isaac Bullard, this peripatetic group originated in Canada and wound its way through Vermont to New York and from there, to Pennsylvania and parts west and south as the Prophet's caravan split into two groups. Bullard bragged that he had not changed his clothes in seven years. He claimed to be the incarnation of the Biblical prophet Elijah, and had abolished marriage among his converts, forced his devotees to pray prostrate on the ground, and had the men eat standing up, sipping their repast through a tube that was inserted into a common bowl of gruel ... all this among other oddities, including the belief that Bullard's infant son was Jesus.

These stories were picked up by the *Wayne Sentinel,* the newspaper in Joseph Smith's town of Palmyra, on May 26, 1826 with the caution:

This fete of folly and delusion, is perhaps worthy of notice, as furnishing a striking instance of the blindness of credulity— the wilderness of fanaticism, and the miserable propensity of the mind, to believe itself possessed of powers which do not belong to humanity.

Later, other authors would link Bullard's group with the Mormons by suggesting that their "fanaticism" and blind allegiance to their "prophet" made them spiritual siblings. This may have been a rather unfair comparison, as Isaac Bullard did not leave behind a new scripture or anything resembling an intellectual accomplishment in the field of exegesis or revelation. Without the Book of Mormon, Joseph Smith may indeed have been just another spiritual impostor or prophet-wannabe, another Prophet Isaac on the road to Ohio; but it was on the strength of that scripture and the method in which it was received—golden plates, shew stones, "reformed Egyptian" and all—that Smith was able to connect so many diverse strains of popular religion and alternative history together. All he needed now was some sort of organization to promote these ideas and help sell the book, which was languishing on the shelves, ridiculed by the mainstream media.

Among his earliest converts, of course, were the scribes who painstakingly took down Smith's dictation, line by tortured line. Oliver Cowdery was one of the first of the Elect. He and Smith had a revelation in May of 1829 that they should be baptized and ordained into the "Aaronic priesthood". So Smith and Cowdery baptized each other and proclaimed their sacerdotal status. By April of the following year, their nascent "Church of Christ" (as it was known then) had about a half-dozen elders and around seventy members. (Fourteen years later, by the time of his assassination, Smith's church had 20,000 followers.)

In June of 1831, Martin Harris became ordained as a High Priest while at the Church's new headquarters in Kirtland, Ohio. It was perhaps the least Smith could do for the man who single-handedly financed the Book of Mormon and who lost his farm and his wife in the process.

The move to Kirtland, Ohio was the beginning of the real launch of Mormonism. Prior to that time Smith found himself facing a great degree of hostility and ridicule in New York. A prophet, after all, is without honor in his own country. He might have quoted the New Testament response to Jesus: "Can any good thing come out of Nazareth?" (John 1:46) Or, we might ask, out of Palmyra, New York?

The move to Kirtland was prompted by a revelation that Smith had concerning establishing Zion—the New Jerusalem—in the territory of Missouri. As it was for Bullard before him, the lure of the west as the Promised Land was irresistible to Smith. It was also probably motivated by a desire to isolate his followers from general society, as the small northeastern towns where Smith grew up and began preaching his new dispensation were filled with people who either knew him or his family, either directly or by reputation. By isolating his flock he would be able to control them more easily, as well as control the way his message was received and interpreted. Not to put too fine a point on it, this isolation can be seen as the motivating factor behind the move of Rev. Jim Jones of the Peoples Temple sect to the jungles of Guyana. Prophets flourish in physical distance from the people who actually knew them before the revelation was received.

The growing opposition to Smith and his teachings was another factor. As Oliver Cowdery began baptizing people into the new Church, the danger of mob violence had begun to increase. Those who remembered Smith's treasure-hunting past were convinced that he was not only a blasphemer but a crook and a confidence man as well. He was arrested as a "disorderly person" but managed to beat the charges and escape the New York area with Cowdery before violence had a chance to escalate.

At the same time, Smith was having trouble with his own Elect. It seems that everyone felt they had a right to use seer stones to divine their own destinies—and that of the new Church—and this meant that Smith's authority would begin to erode. One of his first Witnesses, Hiram Page, claimed that he received divine revelation (through the seer stone) as to the location of the New Jerusalem. Smith quickly reasserted his own position as Prophet and leader of the Church, and claimed a revelation that he was the only true Prophet and that only revelations that came through him were of genuine divine inspiration.

Thus, things were threatening to get out of hand. First, the communities of northwest New York where Smith had grown up and performed his occult experiments with seer stones and magic books were in such opposition to him that violence was possible. He had even been briefly arrested for these activities. Furthermore, his Book of Mormon was not selling. Second, his own people were attempting to exert their own spiritual authority over the Church and the Scripture he had created. Third, others who might have been expected to be sympathetic with Smith's teachings—such as Mordechai Noah—were criticizing him heavily. With all of this opposition, both within and without his organization, he needed a bold move in order to control and direct the energies of his followers and to keep them away from the influences of the press as well as from the courts.

Whatever the actual reasoning behind the move, by January of 1831 the Smith group had arrived in Kirtland, Ohio—outside of Cleveland—and it was there on June 3 of that year that the long-suffering Martin Harris was ordained a High Priest in Smith's Church of Christ. Kirtland would prove to be the first real headquarters of the Mormon denomination, and as such it is still revered to this day by pious Mormons.

And it would be in Kirtland that Joseph Smith got the idea to create his own bank.

Money-digging and treasure-seeking were never very far from Smith's mind. The genesis of Mormonism lay in Smith's early obsession with finding buried treasure. The obsession developed in a place and time that was rife with stories about alchemical transformations as well as an epidemic of counterfeiters. As noted previously there were two themes that ran through the alchemical literature: that of obtaining wealth through the transformation of metals (viewed as a natural process that only had to be hurried-along by the alchemist) and the perfectability of human beings, of which the transmutation of lead into gold was an analogue. It will be seen that Smith eventually abandoned the physical transformation of metals in favor of the idea of human perfectibility.

Before that happened, however, Smith had one more arrow in his mundane treasure-seeking quiver. This involved a return to the Smith family ancestral home in Salem, Massachusetts in 1836.

This unusual event is recorded in several places, notably in the writings of Oliver Cowdery himself who was one of the participants along with Hyrum Smith (Joseph's brother) and Sidney Rigdon.

Sidney Rigdon was the leader of a Christian group in Kirtland numbering about one hundred followers who joined the Mormons along with his entire congregation, thus doubling the size of the Church of Christ that year and becoming an important member of what is called the First Presidency: the leadership group of what would become the Church of Jesus Christ of Latter-day Saints. In 1836 this First Presidency numbered—aside from Smith and Rigdon—Oliver Cowdery and Hyrum Smith. Thus, it can be said that the trip to Salem, Massachusetts involved the entire First Presidency of the Church in what appeared to have been a secret mission.

A man called Jonathan Burgess—a Mormon—notified Smith that there was a treasure buried beneath a certain house in Salem. In the summer of 1836, the entire First Presidency of the Church went to Salem (a considerable distance from Kirtland, Ohio) in order to rent the house under which the treasure was said to be buried. Residency was impossible since the house was fully occupied; they rented rooms close by and then began attempts to gain access to the house (either by renting it or buying it) so they could obtain the buried treasure. Unfortunately, all attempts failed and they were forced to return to Kirtland without having accomplished their task.

That this mission was occult in nature is demonstrated by Oliver Cowdery's diary of the trip, in which he focused primarily on Salem as the scene of the famous witchcraft trials. It was common knowledge among the Smiths that their ancestor—Samuel Smith—was one of those who accused Mary Easty of witchcraft in 1692 and that his testimony had contributed to her sentence of death. For Joseph Smith, this must have seemed like an odd homecoming. He had a pedigree in that town, and was returning to the place where his ancestor had given evidence against a witch only to appear—in secret, as it turned out—as a sorcerer himself.

That Smith's old occupation of treasure-seeking using occult methods was the means by which he figured to locate the exact spot in the house where the treasure was buried is born out by a number of contemporaneous sources, and even prominent members and historians of the LDS Church itself are forced to admit that this was, indeed, the case although some have attempted to give the treasure-seeking a different—more spiritual—spin.

It was less than a year after his empty-handed return to Kirtland from Salem that he came up with another get-rich-quick-scheme, although this one did not involve divining rods or seer stones but a fraud involving land, banking, and the exploitation of the confidence of his investors. This was the Kirtland Anti-Bank Scandal, and the details are incredible.

In 1836, upon the return to Kirtland by the church leadership, it was decided to cash in on the land speculation that was currently rampant in the area by creating a bank. Smith was involved in building the Kirtland Temple, which he intended to be the headquarters of his new religion, and it was an expensive affair that was taxing the financial reserves of the Saints. Smith and his colleagues decided to go the legal route at first in order to set up the bank, and applied to the Ohio legislature for a charter. Several attempts to obtain the charter were defeated in various ways. At the time, the Democratic Party was in control of the Ohio congress and was considerably more fiscally conservative than their Whig counterparts who were in general against banking regulation and in favor of what were then known as "quasi-banks": financial institutions that were part of some other corporation or business and that functioned like banks but which were not covered by a banking charter. As the Ohio congress held the line on issuing such charters in the period 1836–1837, there was no way for Smith to get full legal approval for his operation so he decided to go the "quasi-bank" route.

At the same time, Oliver Cowdery had bank note plates engraved with the title "Kirtland Safety Society Bank." When informed that they could not legally create a bank, he had the plates altered to read "Kirtland Safety Society Anti-Banking Co."

The early Church felt they had the law on their side. There were a number of such "almost" banks in the country, and especially in the state of Ohio. Unfortunately, they also had the reputation of being "wildcat" banks: institutions that were totally un-regulated and answerable to no one. That meant that other lending institutions were loath to deal with the quasi-banks. Obtaining credit would be a problem, as well as any type of money transfer that was based on paper and not on "hard currency." And Smith needed as much hard currency as possible as he was deeply involved in the real estate speculation taking place everywhere in the area.

In order to convince his shareholders that the Kirtland Anti-Banking Company was solvent and a good investment risk, Smith resorted to a ploy that is almost (but not quite) comical in retrospect.

He filled caskets with worthless junk iron and sand, and then covered them with a layer of shiny silver coins, presenting them as evidence that the bank had an enormous amount of silver on hand, which in fact it did not. The outcome was predictable. The bank was insolvent after a year in operation and many people lost their savings when it went bankrupt. (The parallels to the 2008 banking crisis in the United States could not be more striking.)

In fact, the Kirtland Anti-Bank was only one of many such institutions to fail during what would become the 1837 Banking Crisis, which resulted in five years of economic depression in the United States, triggered by President Andrew Jackson's refusal to bail out the Second Bank of the United States with government funds. The Second Bank had been chartered after the charter of the First Bank was not renewed in the aftermath of the War of 1812 and the military expenditures, which nearly bankrupted the young nation, damaged the country's credit standing. Andrew Jackson believed that the only true money was gold and silver and refused to support a national bank, insisting that the states should control their own banking systems. Opponents of Jackson—including the Whig Party, which was supported by wealthy industrialists and bankers—defended the idea of a national bank, of paper currency, and of looser regulations on the private banks. It is interesting to note that many prominent Whigs, including Abraham Lincoln, eventually went on to establish the Republican Party after the collapse of the Whigs in the mid-nineteenth century.

Smith had a hard time recovering from the banking scandal. Many Mormons became disillusioned with Smith and the Church after the huge financial losses they experienced at the hands of their spiritual leaders. As we will see, it would be a pattern that would repeat itself with equally dire consequences in the twentieth century when Salt Lake City (the Mormon capital of the State of Utah) was declared the "fraud capital" of the nation due to investment schemes involving many high-ranking Church officials resulting in the loss of more than two hundred million dollars in the period 1980–1983 alone.

But as Smith was fighting off lawsuits and possible arrest over the failure of the Kirtland Anti-Banking scheme, he had other problems. Mormon settlers in Missouri were being forced out of the territory by the existing population who feared a Mormon takeover of their land. These circumstances were made worse by Smith's revelation that Missouri would be the Promised Land and the New Zion. The situation escalated in 1838, just as the Kirtland Anti-Bank was failing and Smith began losing followers. It developed into what has become known as the Mormon War.

In January of that year Smith and his ally Sidney Rigdon fled Kirtland for Missouri. Arrest warrants were issued, and the possibility of mob violence was also very much in the air. An ad hoc militia had been formed to apprehend Smith and hold him for trial, and Smith had had prior experience with the law.

In 1832, when Smith went to Independence, Missouri to regain control over the fledgling Mormon community there under the leadership of Oliver Cowdery, he was met with hostility. Cowdery felt that Smith had been ignoring him and the "New Zion" in favor of his relationship with Sidney Rigdon. In addition, local non-Mormons were afraid that Smith would try to seize their land in the name of his Church. They also objected to what they felt was his abolitionist stance, as well as Smith's overtures to the Native American population. Thus, Smith had two sources of conflict to resolve: from both within and without his organization. The trip ended badly.

As an angry mob grew, both Smith and Rigdon were seized. They were beaten, tarred and feathered. They barely managed to escape Missouri with their lives. But they did not give up on New Zion.

The Mormons who were left behind had to fend for themselves. They were ostracized by the earlier settlers, and came under increasing pressure to leave. Attempts by the Mormons to convert the Native Americans were stymied by the government which did not recognize their legal authority to proselytize among the tribes; thus another potential source of moral support was denied them. They eventually came to an agreement with the local Missourians that they would not settle in their area and peace was temporarily restored. Suddenly, however, the relationship between the Mormons and the settlers deteriorated to the point that an all-out war began.

Soon after that, Smith's bank had failed. Smith understood that Kirtland was no longer a sanctuary for him or his faith. The temple he had been at great pains and expense to build in that city would have to be abandoned as the two different camps of Mormonism—the Ohio and the Missouri wings—would begin to sever their relationship permanently.

Instead, Smith decided to raise his own army and, basically, invade Missouri.

As the split between the Mormon camps became serious, Smith moved his followers west. The Kirtland temple became the headquarters of the anti-Smith group, and for a time the town of Far West, Missouri was the headquarters of Smith and his loyal followers. The original settlers who felt that the Mormons had violated the agreement they had reached back in 1833 considered this influx of new settlers to the region as a serious threat.

Alarmed by the thousands of new Mormon immigrants, and politically threatened by what could become a huge voting bloc in local elections, the Missourians began to push back.

To make matters worse, Smith found himself excommunicating his original disciples, including among them Oliver Cowdery himself. Cowdery did not welcome Smith's sudden appearance in Missouri after all the work he had been at pains to accomplish to keep the peace in that state and to develop his own power base. By kicking his original disciples out of the Church, Smith had also taken possession of their land which had been bought as Church property. It was a volatile situation and immediately became much worse.

Sidney Rigdon—Smith's new golden boy—came to the defense of Smith and threatened the former Mormons such as Cowdery with physical violence if they did not leave the territory. A secret society was formed, known as the Danites that would have as their task the removal by force of the "dissenting" Mormons.[6] Afraid of being murdered, the newly-excommunicated Mormons fled to other parts of Missouri where they spread their story of Mormon persecution. This had the effect of causing even more paranoia among the Missourians, and they began to arm themselves.

On August 6, 1838, an election day, anti-Mormons gathered at the polling booths to prevent Mormons from voting. A skirmish broke out between the two groups, and the Missourians returned to their homes to get their weapons.

Smith then led a militia of one hundred armed men to the home of a judge who was rumored to have begun gathering his own gang to attack the Mormons. While this event did not turn violent, the die had been cast. Mormon militia groups and the Danite bands began a tug of war with the Missourians that would last all summer and into the fall and which resulted in the pitched Battle of Crooked River on October 25, 1838.

In the previous few months, Mormons had attacked and burned Missourian towns and the Missourians had reacted predictably and attacked Mormon settlements. By October the situation had escalated and Mormon troops, including the Danites, faced a state militia under the command of Samuel Butler, who ordered his men to fire on the Mormon columns. The Mormons took heavy casualties but the state militia fled the battleground, leaving the upper hand to the Mormons.

Reports of the battle—greatly exaggerated—reached the governor of Missouri and he signed an executive order demanding the removal of the Mormons from the state or, barring that, their extermination.

Then on October 30, the Haun's Hill Massacre took place. A large band of more than 200 vigilantes attacked a Mormon encampment in Caldwell County, Missouri. As the women and children fled for the safety of the woods, the Mormon men stood their ground inside a blacksmith's shed and were surrounded by the vigilante force which murdered everyone inside, including

---

6   This would find its modern manifestation in the Church Security department of the LDS Church in the 1980s.

a ten-year-old boy who was killed so that he would not grow up to be a Mormon. A total of seventeen Mormons were killed in the massacre.

The state militia then marched on Smith's new headquarters in Far West, Missouri and demanded the surrender of the Church's leaders. Smith tried to negotiate a peace, but in the end he was arrested and sentenced to death. At the same time, the remaining Mormons at Far West decided to surrender their weapons to the state militia. In response, the militia began destroying the farms and homes of the Mormons, even going so far as to slaughter their livestock and burn down any structures they found. The leader of the militia—General Lucas—informed the Mormons that he had orders to exterminate them all, and he would have done so had they not surrendered. Lucas then went on to hold a court martial of Smith and the other leaders of the Mormon army, including Sidney Rigdon, and found them all guilty of treason. He gave the order to have them executed the next morning, but his order was disobeyed. Instead, the Mormons were bound over to a civil court for an inquiry on charges of treason, murder, arson, etc. and of the sixty men arrested only twelve—including Smith and Rigdon—were charged and imprisoned.

In April of 1839, however, Smith and some of his co-defendants managed to escape custody. The Mormons had already begun their retreat to Illinois, this time under the leadership of Brigham Young, where they would create a new headquarters at Nauvoo, a city they had founded for the purpose. In the meantime, the State of Missouri seized all remaining Mormon land in order to pay for the militia action, warning the Mormons that should they venture back into the State for the purpose of settling there every Mormon man, woman and child would be killed.

This was the state of play in 1839. Driven out of Kirtland, and then forced out of Missouri, Smith was eager to find a place to settle and build his new religion. Sidney Rigdon, who had been such an important influence on Smith and the direction the Church would take, was now losing his position as Smith's right-hand man. This honor went to Brigham Young, whose ascendancy began as Rigdon's declined. It would be Young who would bring the Mormons into what would become the State of Utah after Smith's death.

But it would be Nauvoo that would see the changes that made Mormonism even more scandalous as Smith began receiving revelations there concerning the baptism of the dead and plural marriage, among others. It was also where Smith raised the largest army in the State of Illinois, and from where he would begin his quest for the American presidency. The trajectory that began in the woods of upstate New York and which reached a kind of zenith in Kirtland, Ohio was now plummeting down to earth and an early grave.

The Mormon War in Missouri would continue to haunt Smith for the rest of his days. Having escaped police custody after the 1838 inquiry, he was still a wanted man in the state of Missouri and had to fight extradition. Incorporating the city of Nauvoo gave him certain legal benefits, including the ability to fend off extradition. Had he ever returned to Missouri, however, he would have been captured and jailed, and possibly given a harsh sentence if convicted of the counts of treason and murder that were hanging over him. The death penalty was still an option, as was life in prison.

The need for his own private army was probably based on his feelings of vulnerability after the Missouri debacle. He also had disaffected Mormons to contend with. Some of the men and women who had formed his earliest converts had now turned against him, including Oliver Cowdery who was one of the scribes and who had claimed to have seen the golden plates with his own eyes. But that was almost ten years ago now, and as 1839 came to a close Smith had less than five years to live.

He wasted no time in coming up with newer and grander revelations. Nauvoo was perhaps his most fertile period since the receiving of the golden plates and their ensuing translation. New doctrines came quickly. And so did new converts.

In 1840, Smith proclaimed the doctrine of the baptism of the dead. In order to fully grasp the significance of this practice—which aroused a great deal of controversy in 2012 as revelations were made concerning the Mormon baptism-by-proxy of Anne Frank, of Nazi hunter and Holocaust survivor Simon Weisenthal's family, and of the still-alive but unwitting Elie Wiesel—one has to understand that the Mormon concept of the human soul and the afterlife is quite different from that of Christian and Jewish beliefs.

For instance, there is the concept of pre-mortal existence. This doctrine states that all human beings are co-existent with God, at least in terms of what Smith called "intelligence," a concept possibly borrowed from such sorcerers' workbooks as Agrippa's *Fourth Book of Occult Philosophy* or Francis Barrett's version of the same in *The Magus* where planetary forces manifest as "intelligence" and "spirit." In this scheme, human intelligence took on souls, which then incarnated into bodies as part of a process of spiritual education. As these bodies die, their spirits and intelligences are sent back to one of three grades or degrees of the heavenly afterlife. These are the telestial, the terrestrial and the celestial, with the celestial being the highest heaven. Everyone is assured of immortality and of a continued existence of more or less bliss, depending on how one conducted oneself in this life and what lessons were learned along the way. Evil people are still assured of a heavenly position, after they have gone through a kind of spiritual imprisonment for a time, but they will never attain the highest, celestial, heaven.

Since Smith arrogated to himself the ability to redesign the heavens of the Abrahamic faiths, he also assumed the authority to baptize those who had already died without being able to convert to Mormonism. This practice began as living Mormons expressed the desire to have their deceased loved ones brought into the fold. They would "stand in" for the dead relative and accept the baptism in their name. While that practice may be questionable to many, it was at least conducted with the relatives' approval and participation. Eventually, of course, the practice got out of hand. We will discuss this in more detail in the next chapter but for now it is enough to remember that the much-reported Mormon affinity for genealogical research is connected to this desire to perform baptism by proxy.

Another new doctrine revealed by Smith was that of plural marriage. This came in 1841, but was revealed to only a few members at that time (even though there is considerable evidence that Smith condoned or defended the practice as early as 1833). The theoretical basis for this doctrine is rather obscure, particularly as the Book of Mormon forbids adultery and polygamy and Smith was always publically condemning the practice. As a religious doctrine it did not become official until after Smith's death; however, the number of Smith's plural wives has been documented, although there is still some controversy over the exact number with estimates ranging from about 42 wives to 48.

Plural wifery was related to another Mormon doctrine, that of "sealing." There were two forms of marriage as understood by Mormons: the first was the standard form of heterosexual matrimony of a husband and a wife, a purely secular wedding. This type of union could be temporary, as the Mormons did allow divorce. But there was another type of marriage and this was an eternal form. In this ceremony—conducted at the Temple—a man and a woman were "sealed" forever. It was a state that would continue after death and for all eternity in the afterlife.

None of this implied total monogamy, however. One could be sealed to more than one wife, just as one could be married to more than one woman. In addition, Smith—and some of his successors—would marry the wives of other men, thereby implying that polyandry was also possible according to Mormon doctrine. In fact, one could be "sealed" to a spouse even after that potential mate had died. There are several accounts of women being "sealed" to Joseph Smith after the latter's death.

The practice of plural marriage became public knowledge and official doctrine in 1852, eight years after Smith's death. It would continue as official practice until 1890, when political pressure was brought to bear on the Mormons by the US government as well as by public opinion. To be fair, there were many abuses by those who claimed special dispensation from God to exploit the doctrine for lascivious purposes, and who claimed that "spiritual wifery" meant that they could have their choice of any woman they desired, if even for one night, for they were "married in heaven." While such abuse was punished by excommunication from the Church, the general public associated it with official Mormon policy. After all, once the idea of plural marriage (and "sealing") was accepted how would adultery even be defined? Was there an essential difference between a man claiming to have received direct communication from God that it was acceptable for him to ravish someone else's wife or daughter, and the official policy of Joseph Smith that it was okay for him to do the same thing?

As we will see in the following chapter, not everyone agreed.

In addition to the more scandalous revelations concerning the baptism of the dead and plural marriage, Joseph Smith contributed the idea of a reformed priesthood. He had instituted the priesthoods of Aaron and Melchizedek in the early years of the Church; now he added a more ambitious degree of ordination and initiation, called the "first anointing." This was in 1842, at a time when Smith had become fascinated with the rituals of Freemasonry.

Probably the most antinomian of all the Mormon practices, this new obsession created a secret society within the Church at its highest levels. It was nothing less than an incorporation of Freemasonry—its beliefs and rituals—as the Church's innermost secret. Just as Smith believed he was restoring Christianity to its original meaning and purpose, he also believed he was restoring Freemasonry which he felt had been corrupted over time just as Christianity had degenerated. What many commentators miss in examinations of Mormonism is that the religion is basically a hermetic and occult version of Christianity, a kind of "Christian Kabbalah" ... albeit with presidential candidates and a famous choir. While Mormons themselves may resist this interpretation due to their insistence that they be considered a mainstream Christian denomination, the facts argue otherwise.

In this way, some Christian critics may be excused for claiming that Mormonism is a cult; but they fail to appreciate just what kind of cult it is.

Smith had railed against Freemasonry at a time when the rest of the United States was similarly preoccupied. The Anti-Masonic hysteria began with the disappearance of William Morgan on September 11, 1826 from a town not far from Palmyra, New York where Smith was conjuring angels in the woods. Morgan was a Freemason who was threatening to publish the order's secret rituals, in particular those of Royal Arch Masonry. Before this could take place, he was arrested on a trumped-up charge and held in a jail in town, from where he was abducted by a group of men believed to be Freemasons. He was never seen again.

This incident sparked a public outcry against Freemasonry, and Masonic temples were closed down all over the country in the aftermath. A political party, the Anti-Masonic Party, was formed in 1828 and ran a candidate for president to oppose Andrew Jackson who was himself a Freemason and proud of his membership. Eventually the one-issue party fell apart and its members sought the tweedy embrace of the Whigs.

Anti-Masonic sentiments found their way into The Book of Mormon, which argued against "secret combinations", a way of saying secret societies. Since the book was published in 1830, it found itself in a congenial, anti-Masonic environment. It is one of the reasons why skeptics feel that Smith created the Book of Mormon out of whole cloth, since it so clearly reflected the biases and obsessions of the time in which it was published.

However, as the anti-Masonic furor died down, Smith re-evaluated the importance of Freemasonry to his overall system. (What is not generally known is that he even married William Morgan's widow, and took her as one of his plural wives.)

On March 15, 1842 Joseph Smith was initiated into the first degree—Entered Apprentice—of Freemasonry at Smith's office in town. The following evening he was passed to the Fellow Craft degree and then raised to the degree of Master Mason the same night. This was done in unseemly haste, and there is some question as to why it was allowed but in the absence of a satisfactory explanation we can only assume that there was a political agenda behind this rapid-fire initiation.

Once Smith had received all three degrees he then went on to insist that virtually every Mormon male of appropriate age and standing be initiated as well. By the time these assembly-line initiations were completed there were more Freemasons at Nauvoo than in the entire State of Illinois. This caused some antagonism with the other Freemasons who complained that the Nauvoo Lodge was essentially a diploma mill for Masons. But the die had been cast.

Shortly after publishing the Book of Mormon, Smith had introduced something he called the First Endowment, which involved ordination into the priestly order of Melchizedek, a Smith creation. At Nauvoo, he added the Second Endowment which involved a Masonic form of initiation and the introduction of what has been called disparagingly "magic underwear," the Temple garments that, once bestowed, must never be removed. A glance at their design reveals that the Masonic influence on the Second Endowment ceremony cannot be ignored. (See illustrations on the next two pages.)

The garment bears a reverse L on the right breast, and a V on the left. The reverse L is the Masonic square and the V is the Masonic compasses. In fact, these symbols are described as the square and compasses in Mormon literature. The square and compasses can be seen on many Masonic documents and buildings, such as the following on a Masonic hall in England:

In May of 1842, Smith went on to ordain a number of leading Mormons in the Second Endowment ceremonies. These Mormons were all Freemasons, and included Smith's own brother Hyrum Smith as well as Brigham Young, Hebert C. Kimball, and other famous Mormon leaders. The initiation ceremonies involved secret handshakes, passwords, and a ritual illustrating the Fall from Eden, Adam and Eve, etc. None of this may be revealed to outsiders. No one is permitted as an observer. The

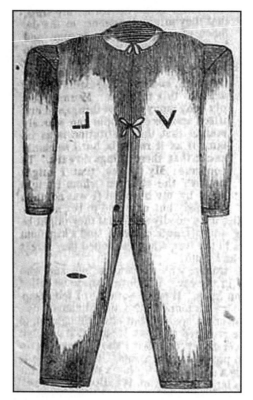

*The "magic underwear" are Temple garments that, once bestowed,
must never be removed. A glance at their design reveals
the Masonic influence on the Second Endowment.*

Second Endowment is structured to be virtually identical to a
Masonic initiation. This was Smith's idea of a "restored" Freemasonry. In fact, it was a restored *Royal Arch* Freemasonry.

The core concept of the Royal Arch degree is that of buried
treasure. According to the ritual, the prospective initiates are
taken to the spot where Solomon's Temple had been destroyed.
Work is about to begin on the Second Temple, and the initiates
are told to begin digging in a certain spot. As they do so, according to *Duncan's Masonic Ritual and Monitor*, they discover "a secret
vault, in which they found treasures of great benefit to the craft."
We find ourselves back once again with the seventeen-year-old
farmboy in the woods outside Palmyra, New York in 1823, being

The traditional Masonic design of the Compasses and Square.

directed by an Angel who will guide him to a certain spot where treasure is buried.

It is tempting to look at this rite in connection with Smith's own life and experience. It had to seem as if the universe itself was speaking to him, in spite of all the hostility that his new scripture, new religion, and new doctrines aroused in the general population. Joseph Smith in 1842 was brought back to the Joseph Smith of 1823, full circle. What had been for him a crucial event—the seminal event—of his life had reappeared, immortalized in a Masonic ritual that had its roots in the England of the eighteenth century. It must have seemed as if the Freemasons a century earlier had predicted—prophesized—the coming of the new Prophet.

Or the explanation may be more prosaic. William Morgan had been threatening to reveal the secrets of the Royal Arch degree at the time Smith was still going to the woods every year to obtain the golden plates. As details of the degree ritual became known, Smith could have easily incorporated them into his personal legend. He, in effect, became the Masonic initiate who literally was told where to find the buried treasure, thus enabling him to build the new Temple and restore both Christianity and Freemasonry thereby.

No matter how they are interpreted, these new developments in the structure of the Church of Jesus Christ of Latter-day Saints would have far-reaching impact on the character of the organization, making it even less approachable for the average Christian and turning it into a secret society with occult rites, strange sexual practices, and bizarre ceremonies and ritual vestments. Instead of making his religion less controversial and more mainstream, Smith increased the strangeness level to an astonishing degree for that time and place. It was as if he was committed to a path of self-destruction.

And to add to the energy levels that were already tuned so high, Joseph Smith then decided to run for President of the United States becoming the first such Mormon candidate.

This was in February of 1844. He announced his candidacy, with Sidney Rigdon as his running mate. His campaign would end with his death four months later. In the meantime, however, Smith's political agenda was far more complex and bizarre than was generally known to outsiders.

Smith had decided that he wanted some degree of independence from the United States government, and formed yet another secret group within the Church. This was the Council of Fifty, and one of its first acts was to crown Smith as the King of the Kingdom of God. Smith had decided that what the world needed was a "theodemocracy" or a God-based democracy with Smith as its head and divine representative. The delusion was sufficiently intense that the Council actually sent ambassadors to various European countries that year. At the same time, Smith was predicting with a great degree of confidence that the United

States government would be overthrown in a matter of years, and that he would be there to pick up the pieces.

At the same time, Smith was still fighting extradition to Missouri where he was wanted for charges of treason, murder and arson. This situation was exacerbated by the attempted assassination of the former governor of Missouri, Lilburn Boggs, by a man identified as a Mormon who was avenging Smith's maltreatment in that state. Boggs, who survived the attempt, demanded Smith's extradition to Missouri for that crime, but the extradition request was eventually pronounced unconstitutional.

In response, Smith had raised the largest militia in the State of Illinois (the so-called "Nauvoo Legion" whose strength in 1844 was roughly 3,000 men, making it almost half the size of the entire US Army!) and had the largest Masonic lodge in the state as well. He was definitely a political power to contend with, and this caused the Illinois legislature many sleepless nights as they pondered ways to contain him.

By announcing for the presidency as an independent—on a platform that included establishing a national bank, free trade, the annexation of parts of Canada, and the redemption of slaves with money from the sale of national land—Smith had thrown down the gauntlet. With tensions rising high, several of his formerly staunch supporters began to defect. Members of the First Presidency of the Church swore out affidavits accusing Smith of polygamy. To make matters worse, in April of 1844 Smith himself had delivered a sermon at a general conference of more than twenty thousand Mormons in which he set forth his doctrine that there are many gods, that men and women may become gods, and that God himself was once a man like any other. The "King Follett" sermon, as it is known (due to its being delivered shortly after the funeral of Mormon elder King Follett) became another hot button topic that threatened to bring down the Mormon Temple once and for all.

Smith may have felt that he was at the zenith of his career in those days. With a huge militia, a massive Masonic presence, the Nauvoo Temple in the process of being erected, and a national stage as he began his candidacy for president, it might have seemed that he was at the height of his career. In actuality, however, his trajectory was in a rapid and fiery descent to earth.

The man who had sworn an affidavit that Smith was a polygamist had then set up his own newspaper in town, the *Nauvoo Expositor*, in which he roundly criticized Smith and the direction the Church was heading. Smith, angry at the growing dissent among his followers, decided that the newspaper should be closed down after only one edition. This was no sooner accomplished then a rival newspaper published an editorial calling for a violent reaction to Smith's autocratic rule in Nauvoo, which was, after all, still a part of the United States.

In a growing state of paranoia tinged with hysteria, Smith declared martial law in Nauvoo on June 18, 1844. The governor of Illinois begged Smith to back down and stand trial at the county seat in Carthage, Illinois for the unlawful destruction of the newspaper and its apparent violation of the First Amendment. At the same time, the governor mobilized the state militia in the event that an all-out war broke out between the Mormons and the other citizens of Illinois.

Smith eventually relented, and surrendered himself at the Carthage courthouse. He was held over for trial on the additional charge of treason, and kept in a second-floor room at the jail, along with his brother Hyrum Smith and two other Mormons.

On June 27, 1844 a mob of men in disguise attacked the jail with the intention of murdering the Mormons. Both Joseph and Hyrum Smith had weapons in their possession, pistols that had been smuggled in to them for their protection. As the mob ascended the stairs, firing at the Mormons, they were answered with return fire. Hyrum was shot and killed immediately. Joseph Smith returned fire, emptying his pistol, and then attempted to jump out the second floor window. He was shot instead and fell to the ground outside the jail, where he was shot again and again. He died on the ground a few feet from the jail.

The assassins were acquitted by a non-Mormon jury.

According to historian D. Michael Quinn, at the time of his death Smith had been wearing a talisman that had been copied from Francis Barrett's *The Magus*. An inspection of this talisman—from a photograph in Quinn's book—shows that the talisman which was intended to ensure success was engraved incorrectly. This is a regular problem among those aspiring magicians for whom the Hebrew alphabet is merely a series of incomprehensible squiggles. The corruption of the Hebrew, Greek and even Latin texts in the sorcerers' workbooks is well-known and plagues the efforts of modern practitioners to recreate the ancient rites. Joseph Smith's talisman was no different.

It was the talisman of Jupiter, a spiritual force that promises success in the courtroom and with judges (Jupiter being the ruling planet of judges). It bears an inscription in Hebrew that should read "Father Jophiel," Jophiel being the ruling Intelligence of Jupiter. However, as Smith's talisman was incorrectly drawn, the inscription reads: "Father, not Jophiel." The Kabbalistic numerology of this mangled phrase then gives us the meanings "cut, divided" and "the end."

And so it was for Joseph Smith.

The Prophet was only thirty-eight years old when he died.

CHAPTER SIX

CHEMICAL WEDDINGS:
THE ALCHEMICAL THEOLOGY
OF JOSEPH SMITH

This day, today
Is the Royal Wedding day.
For this thou wast born
And chosen of God for joy
Thou mayest go to the mountain
Whereon three temples stand,
And see there this affair.

—*The Chymical Wedding of Christian Rosenkreutz*

BEFORE WE PROCEED FURTHER it is necessary to summarize some of the main doctrines of Mormonism which are based on a number of scriptural sources as well as various pronouncements and revelations by Joseph Smith. These have not been added to or subtracted from in any material way by his successors, although there has always been an attempt to reinterpret some of the teachings in order to bring them more in line with government regulations or public opinion. The reinterpretations, however, have never denied the original intent of the scriptural source or revelation, but only made them more or less practical in a modern context. This is an important point to remember, for if the religious or political environment in the United States ever softens in regard to such things as plural marriage the old revelations will become operative. Contemporary Church leaders have said as much, and have been reluctant to abandon the Mormon theology of the mid-nineteenth century. That some Mormon doctrines have not been officially enforced in the present day is not an indication that they have been repealed but only that it is not practical to make use of them.

Sources for these doctrines come from several important scriptures. In addition to the Book of Mormon, there is the all-important *Doctrine and Covenants* (usually referred to as the *D&C* and containing many of Smith's revelations over time), as well as the *Pearl of Great Price* which contains Smith's autobiography and portions of the Biblical Books of Genesis and Matthew that Smith had translated, as well as the Book of Abraham which Smith claimed to have translated from Egyptian hieroglyphics (a claim that was later shown to be false), and the Articles of Faith. Also included among the Mormon scriptures is the King James Version of the Holy Bible.

The prominence given to the King James Bible should not fill any believing Christian with a sense of security, however. European alchemical texts of the eighteenth and nineteenth centuries routinely used biblical analogies for their procedures and often counseled the aspiring alchemist to pray regularly. The same is true for most of the medieval (and later) grimoires. The Bible was considered a source of tremendous wisdom that had been encoded, a belief that had been fostered by the development of Christian Kabbalah in the fifteenth and sixteenth centuries, particularly through the Florentine Academy. In addition, the most notorious of the sorcerers's workbooks were attributed to the authorship of popes, bishops, and even King Solomon himself. The Biblical and ecclesiastical pedigrees were considered essential selling-points for these manuals of spiritual and mundane improvement, in which the Bible was viewed more as a magical instrument and guide to superhuman powers than it was a system of ethics or morals.

This was consistent with the way in which Smith utilized the Bible. Since he had written a new scripture—"correcting" the "errors" in previous scriptures and even performing his own translations of Genesis and the Gospels, as we have mentioned— he had to have viewed the King James Bible with something less than the reverence one would have normally regarded it if one were a minister of Christ. Much in the same way Muslims regard the Bible as an imperfect scripture—a fallible form of the original word of God, which the Qur'an restores to its original meaning—Smith's approach to the Bible acknowledged its primacy and its importance to his own schema, but rejected those aspects of it that did not fit in with his new revelation. It was a jumping-off point, rather than a destination. And just as Muslims regard anyone since Mohammed who claims to be a prophet as a blasphemer and heretic, so too do Christians regard anyone who claims an "additional" revelation, something that would make the Bible's message somehow "better" or "improved."

The revealed text is an object of veneration in the Abrahamic religions. To the Jews, the Tanakh is the perfect text; it can be commented upon and interpreted, but not added to or subtracted from. To the Christians, the Tanakh is the "Old" Testament; it had to be expanded with the addition of the Gospels, the Acts, the Epistles, and the Book of Revelation, i.e. the "New" Testament. To Muslims, the Old and New Testaments tell the story of the prophets that preceded their own, Mohammed and the revelation that he received known as the Qur'an. To Muslims, Mohammed was the "Seal of the Prophets;" there can be no additional prophet. Anyone claiming to be one is either deluded or evil. Or both.

But to Joseph Smith, it was indeed possible to add to the Bible, even to improve it. His approach to the idea of "the text" was in a way cynical and cunning: he created his own. Moreover, he created one that aped the original Bible even to the extent of using the King James vernacular, references to the Temple, to Jesus, and to the lost tribes of Israel. This would seem to indicate that he viewed the original Bible with something bordering on contempt. It was this stratospheric arrogance more than anything else that attracted the animosity of his neighbors. Paradoxically it was also the quality that ensured that his message would survive and, even, prosper.

Kabbalists, occultists and alchemists all pretend to decode the Biblical text. As the perfect document—the handwritten word of God—it contains the mysteries of Nature and of all creation, material and spiritual, if you just knew how to read it and where to look. Smith was aware of this, as were many of his contemporaries. In fact, one could say that the Book of Mormon and the succeeding revelations represented *decoded* portions of the Bible. The theosophy revealed in the ultimate Kabbalistic work—the thirteenth century *Sepher ha-Zohar*—is certainly not to be discovered in a casual reading of the Torah, replete as the *Zohar* is with sexual metaphor and cosmological allusions which are couched in Mosaic language and which use the Torah as a proof text but which are nonetheless not representative of normative Judaism, popularly understood.

While the Book of Mormon does not rise to the sublime intellectual and philosophical level of the *Zohar*, many principles and ideas contained within it and the other related Mormon scriptures, can be associated with similar occult and hermetic principles. The perfectibility of the human being, the various levels of spiritual existence, the esoteric nature of marriage and of the relationship between the sexes, all have their counterparts in Kabbalistic and alchemical texts while they do not appear as such in normative Jewish or Christian scripture.

Thus, while the position of Evangelical Christians vis-à-vis Mormonism as a cult may seem harsh to outsiders, on the basis of theology and church doctrine it will be seen that Mormonism is definitely not a part of mainstream Christianity. And while politicians such as former Massachusetts Governor Mitt Romney may insist that Mormonism is "as American as motherhood and apple pie," that does not mean that it is representative of normative Christian beliefs and most especially not of mainstream Christian practice. One might as well claim that Scientology is Christian, or that it is "as American as motherhood and apple pie." Scientology also had its origins in the United States, and from the same root texts as Mormonism: the sorcerers's workbooks of the Middle Ages and the Renaissance.

So let us take a few moments to look at some of the beliefs of Mormonism as they were revealed to Joseph Smith and codified by the Church of Jesus Christ of Latter-day Saints. It is not the author's intention to condemn these beliefs *per se*, but to demonstrate their antinomian nature for the benefit of those who have heard a lot about Mormonism but who don't understand it.

EXALTATION

Then shall they be gods, because they have no end; therefore shall they be from everlasting to everlasting, because they continue; then shall they be above all, because all things are subject unto them. Then shall they be gods, because they have all power, and the angels are subject unto them.

Doctrine and Covenants, 132:20

Abraham received concubines, and they bore him children; and it was accounted unto him for righteousness, because they were given unto him, and he abode in my law; as Isaac also and Jacob did none other things than that which they were commanded; and because they did none other things than that which they were commanded, they have entered into their exaltation, according to the promises, and sit upon thrones, and are not angels but are gods.

Doctrine and Covenants, 132:37

As the above two selections from the *Doctrine and Covenants* demonstrate, the concept of apotheosis—or becoming god—is part of Mormon doctrine, as is the suggestion that concubinage might also be acceptable so long as God gave the concubines to his followers. In fact, according to the second citation, Abraham and Isaac sit upon thrones in heaven and *are* gods. They are not "godlike" or "godly" or "akin to gods" but are *actual* gods.

This refers to the Mormon concept of *exaltation,* which is virtually identical to apotheosis. According to this teaching, human beings have the ability—through adherence to the law and obedience to the precepts of the Church—to become actual deities. This indicates further that there are those who have already attained this status (such as Abraham and Isaac, above), which implies that there is not one God, but in fact many "Gods." This abandonment of the central tenet of the Abrahamic religions—monotheism—is perhaps the best way to demonstrate that Mormonism is not Christianity in any recognizable form.

Exaltation has its analogues in many spiritual and mystical movements, however. The possibility of becoming a god lies at the heart of some Asian mysticism as well as western ceremonial magic. It may have its origins in Gnosticism, some of whose texts characterize the Creator of this world as a Demi-Urge rather than God the Father. In this tradition, the Serpent in the Garden of Eden was God and his promise to Eve that if she and Adam ate of the Tree of Knowledge they would become "as gods" (Genesis 3:5) was taken as an indication of the human potential for apotheosis.

As we have noted before, alchemy sees humanity as raw material to be refined through a series of psycho-chemical or psycho-sexual processes. The exaltation of lead, therefore, is gold. The exaltation of an average human being would be a god. This theme is reinforced by the idea of Jesus, who was incarnated as a human being, and who promised his disciples "He that believeth on me, the works that I do shall he do also, and greater works than these shall he do; because I go unto my Father" (John 14:12). That anyone would be able to perform "greater works" than Jesus could be taken as implying that a disciple could meet or exceed Jesus's divine status. In alchemy, this reference is taken a step further.

A famous line in the Psalms reads "The stone which the builders rejected has become the chief corner stone" (Psalms 118:22). This line was taken up in Acts as a direct reference to Jesus: "He is the stone which was rejected by you, the builders, but which became the chief corner stone" (Acts 4:11). This is a reference to the words of Jesus himself, who compared himself to the corner stone mentioned in Psalms (Matthew 21:42, Luke 20:17). In alchemy, this was taken to mean that a common substance—something that was found everywhere and generally ignored—was the basis for the entire art, for the Philosopher's Stone: the chemical agent that would transform lead into gold, or the spiritual agent that would transform the common person into a god. It is on this line in Psalms (and the associated references by Jesus in the Gospels) that alchemy and Freemasonry meet. Both are concerned with the perfectability of the human race and with material processes as analogues for spiritual progress. Alchemy uses the language and the environment of the worker in Nature, and employs chemical symbolism; Freemasonry uses rituals of initiation that are based on the Biblical theme of Solomon's Temple and which incorporate architectural symbolism. Yet, in both endeavors the symbols are more than icons or signs; they are the physical proof of the truth of the process, just as the perfected human being is the proof of spiritual attainments.

With exaltation, Joseph Smith was firmly in the camp of the mystics, alchemists, and occultists who held that humans are the raw material of spiritual gold. In mainstream Christianity, obedience to the laws of the Church and repentance for one's sins are the essential elements of redemption. The fulness of redemption is not to be seen in this life, but enjoyed after death in the company of angels. The mysteries of life, death, human suffering, and the incarnation and execution of Jesus are just that: mysteries that can't be known or understood in this life.

To the mystic, however, and especially to the alchemists and magicians, these are mysteries to be solved in this life and redemption is earned and enjoyed while still alive. The western occultist is a kind of Prometheus, stealing fire from the heavens; or perhaps Milton's Mammon in *Paradise Lost* who declares "Better to reign in hell than serve in heaven." This is a rejection of the idea of God as the Chairman of the Board, God as the ultimate Boss who must be blindly obeyed in order to escape annihilation. Rather, this is an insistence on the idea that human beings are co-creators of the universe and that there is nothing to fear from a God who understands everything and who created human beings with the innate desire to attain ever greater degrees of spiritual glory.

While a western occultist or alchemist may find nothing wrong with these sentiments, they are anathema (literally) to those who have a fundamentalist view of Christianity. To them, as to the Jewish mystics of old, there cannot be "two powers in heaven," much less a few billion. To Christians there is a neat cosmological system which is based on ideas of monarchy and autocratic government. There is a single king at the top of the hierarchy, whose word is law and who must be obeyed immediately and without question. This, of course, is God.

Then there are successive layers of the hierarchy accommodating angels, archangels, cherubim, seraphim, etc. and eventually down to human beings, and from there to animals and plants. Creation, in this Christian cosmological system, is not a democracy. God is a leader who must be feared. One can love Jesus and the saints, and pray to them to intercede with God the Father on one's behalf, but one is still a powerless minion of the divine State and subject to the unknowable whim of its leader.

Joseph Smith, who was aware of the promises of the magician and the alchemist as a teenager, would come to doubt those of the preacher and the priest, especially as the occultists spoke of hidden things: secret knowledge and buried treasure, arcane wisdom and mysterious wealth. As we can see from the story of his life, it was not in his nature to accept the vaguely-defined "will of God" and hope for the best, but to try to make things happen himself. For a young boy with little formal education and a family always on the verge of financial ruin at a time of tremendous economic uncertainty, there were few avenues available to him. Religion promised succor and hope, but at some undefined "later." Smith needed "now."

The ceremonies of ritual magic place the operator—the magician—at the center of a circle that symbolizes safety and completion. The magician is the god of his creation. He is able to order about the spiritual forces of good and evil, just as God does from his throne in heaven. He is a priest, but armed with the symbols of political and military authority: the wand and the sword, respectively. He shouts, he orders, he commands ... and the invisible flying things of the ether are compelled to respond and to obey.

Joseph Smith, in his own process towards exaltation, was just such a magician. He used religion to pursue political and military ends. He was the general of his own army, and a candidate for American president; he was also the King of the Kingdom of God on earth. He ordered, he shouted, he commanded. He began by scratching a circle in the dirt in the Palmyra forest, and then ended by commanding legions of armed men. The outward emblems of his spiritual authority were there: Church, State, Army.

And he promised all of this to his followers. "Greater works than these ... "

THE THREE HEAVENS

In addition to a plurality of gods and, as we shall see, a plurality of spouses, there was a plurality of heavens in Smith's cosmology. Again, in this he was not so different from the magicians and Kabbalists that preceded him. The *merkavah* mystics of fifth and sixth century CE Judaism spoke of seven heavens. The cosmological systems of Swedish mystic and philosopher Emanuel Swedenborg may have also influenced Smith, as historian D. Michael Quinn has suggested, since Swedenborg also discusses the idea of heavenly marriage which predates Smith's own views on marriage in the afterlife.

To Smith, there are three separate heavens, or "degrees of glory": the lowest, or "telestial," followed by the terrestial heaven and then the celestial—or highest—heaven. The assignment to the appropriate degree or heaven depends on how one conducted one's life while alive and while in an intermediary state known as the "spirit world." The "telestial"—a word created by Smith—was the place where most people would eventually find themselves. Since God does not consign anyone to hell in Smith's theology, even compulsive sinners will one day find themselves in the telestial kingdom. Those who refuse God and refuse his glory, however, become "Sons of Perdition" and find themselves in the "outer darkness" along with those demons who revolted against God in the time before Creation. This is construed as a voluntary exile from God, and not as a judgment from God. The vast majority of souls, however, will go to one of the three heavens and the majority of those will be found in the first, or lowest, telestial heaven. Those who did not accept Christ while alive will have to wait in "spirit prison" for one thousand years, until the millenial period is over, before ascending to the telestial realm.

The second level or degree of glory is the terrestial heaven. Most of those who arrive here wavered in their acceptance of Jesus in their lifetime, but eventually accepted him.

The third or highest degree of glory is the celestial heaven. This is for those who not only accepted Jesus completely in their lifetimes but who followed all the Church's rules and regulations faithfully their entire lives. The fortunate inhabitants of this degree have become literal gods and goddesses; have attained the apotheosis or exaltation.

The approach to the three degrees of glory is an indirect one, however. After death, according to Mormon theology, one enters the "spirit world." In the spirit world are two possible waiting rooms. The first is Paradise, where souls wait in happiness for their bodily Resurrection. The second is Spirit Prison, where souls who have sinned against Jesus must suffer while they wait for their own Resurrection. Resurrection is understood as the renewal of the physical body. At the time of death, spirit and body separate. The spirit goes to the spirit world, and the body waits for the Resurrection when it will be reunited with its spirit.

At that point there is a Final Judgment as to which of the three heavens the resurrected will go. There is also the chance that the resurrected person will go to the outer darkness, having been given the chance to accept Jesus and having rejected him anyway. That is the only way one can find oneself in eternal damnation: by choosing it.

There is one more realm to this complex Mormon cosmology, and that is the "Pre-Mortal World." According to Mormonism, everyone has already existed before physical birth. They are sent to the world and pass through a "veil of forgetfulness" on their way to incarnation. The concept of a Pre-Mortal World has its counterpart in the Post-Mortal World or the Afterlife.

Mormons refer in their writings to Pre-Mortal and Post-Mortal existences with elan:

> In the premortal realm, spirit sons and daughters knew and worshipped God as their Eternal Father and accepted His plan by which His children could obtain a physical body and gain earthly experience to progress toward perfection and ultimately realize his or her divine destiny as an heir of eternal life. The divine plan of happiness enables family relationships to be perpetuated beyond the grave. Sacred ordinances and covenants available in holy temples make it possible for individuals to return to the presence of God and for families to be united eternally.
>
> —LDS President Gordon B. Hinckley,
> *"The Family: A Proclamation to the World,"*
> *September 23, 1995.*

This single paragraph from a relatively recent proclamation by the fifteenth president of the Church of Jesus Christ of Latter-day Saints encapsulates many of the ways in which Mormons differ significantly from other Christians. Aside from the weird "spirit sons and daughters" terminology, the concept of the premortal realm is front and center. We all, according to Mormon doctrine, pre-existed in our current genders. We incarnated as part of a process by which we will gain perfection. Our family relationships will continue after death, but only if we have received the ordinances and covenants in the holy temples of the Mormon church. Otherwise it seems that we are out of luck.

The idea of perfectability is alien to normative Christian doctrine. All a Christian can hope for is to be "saved" from eternal damnation by living according to God's laws and abstaining from sinful thoughts, words and deeds. This is not "progressing towards perfection", but simply keeping your nose clean and staying out of trouble.

But perfectability is central to alchemical and occult belief and practice, otherwise there would be no alchemy, no secret rituals, no initiatory societies, no esoteric teachings. As we have been seeing all along—and contrary to official Mormon dogma—Joseph Smith's religion is an occult order, made even more so by his adoption of Masonic ritual as an overlay to his treasure-seeking, ceremonial magic origins.

Another interesting aspect of the Mormon heaven system is the possibility of marriage in the afterlife. As mentioned previously, spouses on earth can be "sealed" for eternity in heaven, even after one of them has already died. This type of "spirit marriage" is not unique: some Chinese ethnicities practice this form of marriage (*minghun* in Mandarin) when a person has died as a bachelor. In order to provide him a wife in the afterlife, his family arranges a marriage with a suitable dead woman and the marriage rites are performed as if both are still alive, after which the woman's corpse is moved to a grave next to her "husband". In some cases, a living woman is married to a dead man. In that instance, the wife remains faithful to her dead husband (takes a vow of celibacy in this life), and visits his grave like a normal dutiful spouse every year, etc. The difference between the Asian concept of spirit marriage and the Mormon version is that the former is a strategy for ensuring that the deceased is cared for in the afterlife, and to avoid the return of the spirit of the dead bachelor to haunt his family. It is a prophylactic mechanism that serves a purpose. In the case of the Mormon "spirit marriages" there seems to be no such purpose being served. The motivation for instituting such a practice must remain obscure, unless we look once again to occult sources.

This is another instance in which Swedenborg and Smith agree, as Swedenborg felt that marriage did, indeed, take place in heaven and that even the angels got married. The use of terms like "spirit world" and even "spirit prison" imply a degree of familiarity with Swedenborg as well as with the nascent Spiritualist movement which did not begin officially until after Smith's death but which started in the same "Burned-Over" district of New York State as Smith's religion. The ideas of Swedenborg as well as Franz Mesmer (from whom we get the term "mesmerism" as a form of hypnosis) were very much in the air at the time and were part of the public discourse in the 1830s and 1840s. Is this once again evidence of Smith's deliberate incorporation into his doctrine of those ideas and themes that were prevalent in the time and place he lived, specifically those *alternative* ideas and themes?

If so, one would be hard-pressed to come up with a similar precedent for his concept of plural marriage.

CHEMICAL WEDDINGS

I am using the term "chemical wedding" to refer to the type of mystical marriages that Smith's doctrine supports and encourages because of the similarities between Mormon ideas on the one hand and alchemical concepts relating to the *soror mystica,* or "sister in the mysteries" on the other.

Smith's early attempts to obtain the golden plates were stymied due to an injunction by the Angel Moroni that he was to bring his oldest brother Alvin with him on the attempt scheduled for September 22, 1824. However, Alvin died suddenly in November of 1823 and was thus unable to assist Joseph in the quest for the golden plates, so the visit to the Hill Cumorah the following September 22 came to naught. He was told by the Angel Moroni to return to the hill on the same night the following year with "the right person" although Moroni never identified who that person might be.

In 1825, Joseph Smith met Emma Hale, the daughter of a man in Harmony, Pennsylvania, whose brother had hired Smith to help him find buried treasure using his seer stone. Smith fell in love with Emma Hale and proposed marriage, but her father refused the match on the grounds that Smith was a stranger and had no visible means of support.

Smith returned to the Hill Cumorah in 1826 with another diviner, but that also came to nothing.

In January of 1827, Smith and Emma Hale eloped and were married. He took his new wife with him to the Hill Cumorah on

— autumnal Equinox

September 22, 1827 and on that night (while Emma waited in a wagon and prayed) the Angel Moroni finally allowed him to retrieve the golden plates. Emma Hale was "the right person" as Smith had suspected for more than a year.

Not very much is made of this incident, yet it was a critical development in Smith's personal mythology. The Angel Moroni insisted that he bring the "right person" with him in order to retrieve the plates, but the "right person"—in this case, Emma Hale—had nothing directly to do with the finding or retrieving of the plates. She remained some distance away, where she could not view the event, and prayed.

What, then, was the point of the exercise?

We have to return to the original demand of the Angel that Joseph bring his older brother Alvin with him the following year. Alvin was Joseph's oldest brother and an important member of the family whose work ethic was essential to the family's survival. Alvin represented sobriety and capability. As his younger brother, Joseph probably looked up to him and wanted his approval and validation. He would have been a "right person", someone Joseph could trust and someone with whom he had great affection. His death a few months after the first visit to the Hill Cumorah would have come as a terrible blow, and it is no wonder that it took Joseph three years before he could provide another "right person." It is interesting that neither of his parents or his other siblings would make the cut, even though both his father and his brother Hyrum would become Mormons.

Smith claims he knew immediately upon meeting Emma Harris that she was the "right person" the Angel required. A skeptical response would be that Smith had fallen for Emma and decided that she would be the person he would take to the Hill Cumorah to retrieve the plates. A kinder response might be that he fell in love with Emma after he realized that she was the "right person" mentioned by the Angel. Regardless of how this came about, the fact that he took a woman—his wife—to the Hill for this seminal event in American religious history is suggestive of how he related to women during the rest of his life. His views on marriage, plural marriage, and sealing are the ideas that non-believers first encounter in any discussion of Mormonism as they have become so scandalous.

This is not the place to go into a deep analysis of Smith's psychological or emotional makeup, or his motives in marrying Emma (Harris) and—at last count—some forty or so other women. What will concern us now is the nature of his spiritual ideas about women and especially of the relationship between men and women, and how these ideas reflect profound alchemical themes about the power of sexual union.

It is entirely possible that western alchemy had its origins in the Tantric mysticism of India, which also influenced to a great degree the Daoist alchemical practices of ancient China. Simply put, alchemy in this context uses the terminology of the chemical laboratory as a way of describing psycho-sexual processes that lead to spiritual transformation. In Chinese alchemy, the relationship is made obvious by the depiction of chemical apparatuses as organs of the human body.

Any reference to popular European alchemical texts with their strange illustrations of men and women—usually depicted as kings and queens—in various stages of marital embrace will assure the reader that there is a sexual component to alchemy or perhaps, an alchemical component to sexuality. In India, the practice of Tantra is a manifestation of ideas concerning the psycho-spiritual relationship between males and females, either as human beings or as gods and goddesses or in more abstract terms such as shakti, lingam and yoni, etc. The practitioners of Tantra, known as tantrikas, employ the language of sexuality in both directions, i.e., using sexual allegories to describe physical or spiritual processes as well as using physical or spiritual allegories to describe sexual processes. The beauty of Tantra and its associated "twilight language" is that it is a discussion about the very basis of creation, matter, and energy and thus can be used to describe a laboratory process as well as a temple ritual. Tantric concepts and terminology are to religion and the spiritual experience what mathematics is to science: a universal language.

In this tradition, the role of the woman is paramount. She is the source of energy, of divine power, of shakti. While the male may seem to be the dominant player in this production, it is more in the style of a lion-tamer with the lioness. Without the lion, the tamer is nothing. Without the tamer, the lion is still a lion.

Sex in this context is a unity of more than the physical man with the physical woman. The human bodies are carriers of something divine, something ineffable which must be sensed and cultivated with great care. The sexual act mimics the act of Creation itself which, in the Tantric view, was the result of the union between the god Shiva and his female consort, the goddess Uma or Parvati.

In western alchemy, these concepts are given different names but they refer to the same forces. There is much talk of a white eagle and a red lion, for instance, representing the male and female elements respectively (in some texts; in others the gender identities are reversed). In other cases, there is simply talk of a Bride and a Bridegroom, allusions perhaps to the Song of Solomon in the Bible which may, itself, be a mystical text intended for decoding by an "enlightened" or "initiated" reader. In any event, what the alchemists call the *coniunctio oppositorum* or the "union of opposites" is a necessary step in the process. Known as the *hieros gamos*, or sacred wedding, this concept has a long tradition dating back to the earliest recorded rituals of the Middle East when the king of Babylon—for instance—would embrace a goddess once a year in a special chamber at the top of the sacred ziggurat.

A few famous alchemists and occultists worked as married couples. Thomas Vaughan and his wife Rebecca are one such example, and their alchemical experiments in seventeenth century England probably had a heavy sexual (or at least biological) component, as one can see from Vaughan's published work.

But perhaps the best-known text that discusses the alchemical process in terms of a wedding is the *Chymical Wedding of Christian Rosenkreutz*, first published in German in 1616 and later in English by 1690. This work treats alchemy from the standpoint of a series of initiatory ordeals, all revolving around a marriage and a massacre. Christian Rosenkreutz is, of course, the hero of the Rosicrucian Society: a secret order said to have announced itself a few years before the appearance of the *Chymical Wedding* in a series of mysterious manifestos.

The Rosicrucian manifestos—the *Fama Fraternitatis* and the *Confessio*—created tremendous excitement in Europe at the time. The story was that a seeker after wisdom, Christian Rosenkreutz, traveled throughout Europe and the Middle East in search of lost knowledge. He returned to Europe sometime in the fifteenth century and died there after living a long life and attracting to himself a handful of companions whose identities would remain forever secret. They were allowed to help people as doctors only, and to keep a low profile and not to charge for their services. They were known as "Rosicrucians" after the family name of their founder, but that in itself was a code. Christian Rosenkreuz—or "Christian Rosey Cross"—was an obvious reference not only to Christianity and the Cross but also to a specific image of a rose superimposed on a cross, an image that some later occultists claimed was a reference to the "great secret" of western alchemy: the union of the male (the cross) with the female (the rose). The fact that a rose and cross emblem could be found on the heraldic device of Martin Luther was another clue that the Rosicrucians were believers in the Protestant Reformation and were therefore opposed to the excesses of the Catholic Church.

The third "Rosicrucian" document, the *Chymical Wedding*, took these ideas much further. There has been some scholarly analysis of this virtually incomprehensible work, representing attempts to discover political or historical elements within it as well as the purely initiatory structure. Rather than delve too deeply into its story, it is enough for the present to recall that at heart it is about a royal wedding and the ensuing spiritual transformation of the married couple. It is a "chemical" wedding, i.e., a union of elements that produces a third substance that is more than the sum of its parts.

Since sexual reproduction results in the incarnation of a spirit in a physical sheath or body—a human child—the implications for any sex act are enormous from both a religious and an occult point of view. The two partners are seen as divine participants in the original yet ongoing act of Creation. The parents of the Prophet Muhammad were the unwitting agents of a new religion that would eventually count more than a billion adherents in the world. Yet the parents of Hitler were the unwitting agents of the destruction of more than 50 million human beings and untold suffering, including nearly eradicating the Jewish and Gypsy peoples. In both cases, the sexual act was the same in all its essentials: a man and a woman united in sexual embrace resulting in male ejaculation and female impregnation. But there was no anticipation of the actual outcome of these acts, no indication that one sexual act would produce a prophet and the other a monster.

In alchemical terms, the end result—whether saint or sinner—is always in view. The process is controlled and the outcome is assured. The alchemist may fail along the way, and may never attain the desired goal of the Philosopher's Stone or the Elixir of Life; but in any event the successful accomplishment of the quest would never produce a monstrous offspring but the spiritual "gold" that is promised to the pure.

In Joseph Smith's theology, the spiritual marriage that takes place under the rubric of "sealing" will always result in a divine union. The couple will find each other in heaven and will be paired forever. There is, however, no particular emphasis on the reproduction of spiritual children in heaven. Since all mortals had a pre-mortal existence it stands to reason that in the post-mortal phase there would be no reproduction, no "additional" souls. The marriage itself is the goal; children are products of the mortal phase and are important insofar as they represent God's "spirit children" incarnating in this world in order to proceed on towards the post-mortal phase. If children are not to be produced in the post-mortal existence then there is the implication that the role of women in heaven is somewhat reduced; it is certainly changed Fertility is not a feature of the afterlife, even though marriage is revered as sacred and eternal. The role of the exalted Mormon as a god or goddess is therefore not as a creator; as with most Abrahamic versions of heaven, the role of human inhabitants of the celestial realm seems to be as observers rather than actors in the cosmic drama. While the alchemical goal is usually limited to the attainment of the Philosopher's Stone and the implied perfection of the human agent—the "exaltation" of Joseph Smith's theology—in the (original?) Tantric context the initiates become united with the god and goddess and become part of the ongoing cosmic dance.

This is the essential difference between a linear form of spiritual time as it is understood in many western religions and a cyclical form of time as found in many Asian cosmological systems. In the west, there is a beginning and an end to spiritual evolution. Thus, the idea of "children" becomes superfluous once apotheosis is attained. Creation, in the west, will eventually come to a stop at the End of Days. All scores will be settled; all debts paid, all tickets punched. Regardless if one is a Mormon and believes in the perfectability of humans to the point that they become gods and goddesses, or if one believes in the normative Judeao-Christian-Islamic sense that human beings are submissive to a single God and desire only to enter Paradise at the end of life, there is an end-point. There may be sex—viz. the famous legends of virgins awaiting the soldier who dies in *jihad*—but there is no pregnancy. It is, in short, a male (or, perhaps, a human) fantasy of heaven.

Which is not to say that heaven is without children in the Mormon framework. Those who die before the age of eight go directly to heaven, whether they have been baptized or not. Baptism in Mormon practice is reserved for those who willingly and consciously make the decision to become baptized, and thus children are not baptized until they have reached the age where it is assumed they can make a conscious choice. That particular idea, however, is not applied in the case of proxy baptism, or baptism of the dead, in which case a family member makes the choice on behalf of a deceased ancestor.

In 2012 there was an ongoing scandal concerning the practice of proxy baptism. In this case, it was revealed that the deceased relatives of Holocaust survivors—including Anne Frank—had been baptized in the Mormon temple. There was outrage from some members of the Jewish community, and perhaps rightly so due to the arrogance and insensitivity of the Mormon clergy involved, but it begged the question: is such a "baptism" valid in any meaningful sense of the word? Do people who object to having their dead relatives baptized this way only wind up acknowledging the efficacy of the rite? Does that make them de facto believers in the mechanisms of Mormon ritual, the so-called ordinances?

ORDINANCES AND COVENANTS

What to a Roman Catholic is a sacrament—baptism, penance, communion, confirmation, matrimony, ordination, extreme unction (last rites)—are to a Mormon the "ordinances." The most important of these (the "saving ordinances") include baptism, confirmation, ordination into the priesthood of Melchizedek, the endowment, and the marriage sealing as well as the sealing of children to their parents. (As in Roman Catholicism, only men may be ordained as priests.) To the Mormons, the ordinances must be applied to a human body; in other words, the ordinances can only take effect on a physical form. This is not quite the same as the Catholic sacraments which are supposed to mark the soul and not the body (a doctrine which has given rise to the movement to ordain women as priests if gender is believed to be a feature of the physical body and not the soul). Thus, in order for a person to be baptized after death, there is a requirement that there be a human stand-in for the baptism. Hence the term "proxy baptism." The steps that need to take place to perform the proxy baptism collectively is known as "temple work."

One does not have to baptize one's own family members only. There is a clear statement in one of the Mormon manuals that states:

You may do this work in behalf of your ancestors and others who have died. Acting for them, you can be baptized and confirmed, receive the endowment, and participate in the sealings of husband to wife and children to parents.

—"Temples" in *True to the Faith: A Gospel Reference*, p. 172

As you can see, all of these ordinances may be performed on behalf of those to whom one is not related at all. That is why it was possible for Mormon priests to baptize Jews who had died in the Holocaust, such as Anne Frank, without being asked to do so by a relative of the deceased.

One of the most important of all the ordinances is the Temple Endowment. It represents a full membership in the LDS Church and must be undertaken by everyone prior to their 21st birthday and especially before one is permitted to go on the virtually compulsory mission assignments. Women should receive the Endowment before they are married.

In order to receive the Endowment one must first obtain a "Temple recommend." This is a document that attests that the potential candidate is spiritually fit to enter the temple and is basically in a state of grace. There are interviews of the candidate before he or she is considered acceptable, and then the recommend is signed and is good for two years.

The ceremony begins with the ordinance of ceremonial washing and anointing. After this, the candidate removes all clothing and puts on the famous "Mormon underwear", a ritual garment which from that point on is never taken off. As we saw earlier, this garment has Masonic symbols embroidered on it. It is pure white, as are all items of clothing worn in the temple. During the Endowment ceremony a white robe is worn over the undergarment.

The participant is then introduced to a series of enactments of various scenes that are believed essential to understanding the relationship of humans to God. This includes a re-enactment of Creation and of certain dialogue between Adam and

Eve. If one keeps in mind all that has already been said about the "chemical wedding", one can see that Adam and Eve represent the first "married couple" in Biblical history and that they lived in Paradise, so the theme of a sealed marriage in heaven is prefigured in the story from Genesis.

This is accompanied by instruction in certain secret gestures and handshakes as well as passwords, all in the style of Masonic ceremony. The candidate is then tested in his or her knowledge of these secrets and in their understanding of the meaning behind them (which is expected to change over time). They are then brought before a veil which separates them from God's presence as more questions are asked. After they are satisfactorily answered, the veil is lifted and they spend some time in the presence of God in heaven.

This ritual is experienced many times in the life of a pious Mormon. The first time occurs, as mentioned, when the Mormon is still quite young. After that, however, he or she is expected to undergo the ritual again at a later date, on behalf of someone who was not able to hear the Mormon teachings and receive the Endowment themselves. In other words, they will go through a ceremony identical to their first but as proxy for an ancestor or for some other person. This will happen again and again during an average Mormon's life.

This is the ritual that was created by Joseph Smith at Nauvoo, Illinois after he had been initiated into Freemasonry. The Temple Endowment ceremony represents a "restored" version of the Masonic initiation. Until recently, the instructional portion of the initiation involving the creation of the world, Adam and Eve, etc, was performed by live actors in the manner of Masonic ritual. Lately, however, some of this instruction is given in a video format in the temple, but the secret gestures, handshakes, and passwords are still taught live.

During the Endowment ceremony certain "covenants" are given. A covenant in Mormon parlance means an oath or a commitment to a certain course of action. Ordinances are accompanied by covenants, which is a way of saying that the sacraments are accompanied by vows. Normally, these covenants are promises to live a spiritual life, conscious of one's actions, and to maintain a strong relationship to the church, the community, and one's family. The sacred undergarment is a further reminder of these covenants and a protection against the temptations of the flesh.

The Temple Endowment ceremony is secret. No outsider may witness and certainly not participate in the Endowment (or even gain access to the Temple itself). This level of secrecy is unique, since it applies to every able-bodied member of the faith. Imagine secret rituals for Catholics or Presbyterians; for Muslims or Jews. It is a survival of the Masonic lodge environment with which Smith became entranced in the last years of his life. Masonic ceremonies are also performed in a temple; there is special clothing (the Masonic apron being the most familiar); oaths are taken to keep the rituals secret; and secret passwords, handshakes and gestures are taught. One can safely say that none of this exists in normative Abrahamic practice. In a sense, every Mormon is a kind of Freemason. The Temple Endowment is not reserved for a priesthood but is available to everyone and everyone is encouraged to undergo the rite many times in their lives. Just as the Masonic initiations are a reworking of the story of the building of Solomon's Temple as it appears in the Bible, so too is the Mormon Endowment ceremony a reworking of Genesis. Both Masons and Mormons take a basic theme from the Old Testament and re-imagine it.

Religion, mysticism, magic and alchemy—plus history and archaeology—were components of Joseph Smith's personal sandbox in which he played to his heart's content, oblivious of how he was kicking sand in the other kids' eyes; creating a mountain of alternative versions of everything more like a science-fiction or fantasy novelist than a spiritual leader. There is no doubt that the Book of Mormon was a tremendous accomplishment, especially considering the short period of time in which it was created and by a young man who had little in the way of formal education. The ensuing "revelations" that codified such concepts as the baptism of the dead and plural marriage, as well as the temple endowment, only increased the antinomian aspect of his restoration project.

The question we have to ask ourselves is: does any of this make Joseph Smith any less of a prophet than, say, Moses who created a new religion based on bits and pieces of whatever was available at the time, fueled by inspiration and imagination? Moses was also a political leader and a military commander. Moses also had a hard time finding a home for his new movement. Moses also had plural wives.

And Moses also died before he could reach the Promised Land.

Agendas

CHAPTER SEVEN

THE PROMISED LAND,
IN THIS WORLD AND THE NEXT

And it came to pass that I beheld many multitudes of the
Gentiles upon the land of promise; and I beheld the wrath
of God, that it was upon the seed of my brethren; and they
were scattered before the Gentiles and were smitten.

And I beheld the Spirit of the Lord, that it was upon
the Gentiles, and they did prosper and obtain the land for
their inheritance; and I beheld that they were white and
exceedingly fair and beautiful, like unto my people before
they were slain.

—1 Nephi 13:14–15

THE ASSASSINATION OF JOSEPH SMITH IN 1844 did not result
in an eruption of violence against non-Mormons, as was feared.
Instead, Brigham Young took over the leadership role of the
Church and became in the process the second-most important
Mormon in history after Smith himself. It was Young who led the
Saints into the Promised Land, accomplishing what Smith in his
lifetime tried and could not.

Brigham Young (1801–1877) was born, like Smith, in Vermont. He also held a variety of jobs in his pre-Mormon career,
such as blacksmith and craftsman. But in 1830 he read the Book
of Mormon and joined the denomination, becoming a missionary to Canada by 1832. He traveled to Kirtland, Ohio and
became one of the original Twelve Apostles—the "Quorum of
the Twelve"—in 1835, becoming its president in 1840.

Young was energetic and devoted. He performed missionary
work in England for the Mormons and in 1838 he helped the
beleaguered Missouri Mormons escape to Illinois. His abilities as

a leader were unquestioned, and when Smith was assassinated he was the logical candidate as successor.

There had been no clear-cut policy of succession in the Church. Most thought it likely that Smith's brother Hyrum would be the successor except that Hyrum was murdered along with Smith. (It is interesting to note that Hyrum's name is the same as that of the central personage in the Masonic initiations, Hiram Abiff, who according to Masonic lore was one of the architects of the Temple of Solomon and who was also slain.) Smith had other brothers, none of whom was considered appropriate as the new leader. One of Smith's sons by Emma Harris Smith was Joseph Smith III, but he was too young at the time of Smith's death. Eventually the Church elders agreed that Brigham Young would make the best successor to Smith and he was duly elected and appointed. (Joseph Smith III would go on to run the Reorganized Church of Jesus Christ of Latter-day Saints in 1860: a competitor of Young's group.)

It was the role of Emma Harris Smith that caused the most immediate controversy, for she despised Brigham Young and would have nothing to do with the Church after the death of her husband. The reasons for this may have everything to do with plural marriage.

To the end of her life, Emma Smith insisted that her husband did not practice any form of polygamy or plural marriage, even when presented with evidence that would disprove her position. Yet, the policy of plural marriage was in place as early as 1831 when the Smiths had only been married for four years. It was a secret policy, to be sure, at least at the time. Smith had confided the revelation to Brigham Young among a few others (and conceivably not to Emma), and Young took it very much to heart.

That Smith had plural wives is beyond doubt; the only controversy is their number, with some estimates beginning around 20 to 25 wives, with others ranging up to the forties and even the eighties. The problem with the accounting is based on the lack of marriage certificates or any form of actual documentation. Plural marriage was illegal in the United States and there would have been no courthouse in the land that would have issued this type of paper (for the sake of the trees, if nothing else). But Smith was always surrounded by a number of very young women—many of his wives were under twenty years of age—and in some cases they even lived with the Smith couple. Rumors abounded that one of the reasons Smith had to leave Kirtland was due to some difficulties over plural marriage, and he definitely had an affair with a servant girl at the time (which he defended, saying it was not adultery since he had married her according to Mormon doctrines).

It is entirely possible that Emma Harris's denial of her husband's plural marriages stemmed from a desire to disown the other women and to forbid them any part of the Smith estate. Emma was also in a legal tussle with Brigham Young over the issue of personal property versus Church property, and Young was a strong supporter of plural marriage.

Another issue, however, may have been even more personal.

On September 28, 1843 she and her husband Joseph Smith took part in the very first "Second Anointing" at Nauvoo.

The "First Anointing" takes place during the Temple Endowment ceremony in which the candidate is washed and anointed before proceeding to the rest of the ritual. This anointing recognizes that the candidate is on his or her way to becoming a priest or priestess, a king or queen, a god or a goddess ... in other words, towards exaltation.

The Second Anointing, however, is far more serious and the details of the ritual are a closely held secret. To this day, the LDS Church refuses to disclose how many Mormons have received the Second Anointing, although the number is probably quite small in comparison to the total membership. The reason for this is that the Second Anointing is equivalent to the *hieros gamos* or alchemical wedding. In this ritual, the husband and wife become a king and queen ... they become gods on earth and are assured of—*guaranteed*—their exaltation in heaven.

Emma Smith and Joseph experienced this ceremonial transformation only nine months before Smith's assassination. It is difficult to imagine a ritual with profounder implications for the parties involved, and even more difficult to reconcile this experience with the concept of plural marriage. It could be that Emma Smith took the ritual very seriously, interpreting this form of "celestial marriage" as a stamp of eternal monogamy even though it is doubtful that Joseph Smith saw it the same way.

A more cynical analysis might be that Smith's multiple marriages with their intimations of infidelity might have inspired Smith to create this ritual in order to mollify his wife and allay any fears she might have had about their marital state. Regardless of his motivations, however, the Second Anointing is perfectly consistent with the way in which he was developing and improving upon his original hermetic, alchemical and occult, project. He was designing a ritual form of the apotheosis of his spiritual revelations. It was an act of ceremonial magic, an extension of Freemasonry's male-centered initiatory structure into a sexual field that included women as partners in the highest attainable degree. He took the quiet intimations of human perfectability present in the Masonic degree system and blatantly claimed the ability to confer male and female divinity in this lifetime.

Nine months later almost to the day he would be murdered. In a sense, the exaltation he proclaimed in September resulted in his death and subsequent immortality in June, after a period analogous to pregnancy. Smith gave birth to himself as a god, just as previously he had given birth to himself as a prophet.

In the end, Emma Harris Smith left Mormonism and married a non-Mormon. She would eventually return to the fold when her son Joseph Smith III began running the Reorganized Church of Jesus Christ of Latter-day Saints, but that might also have been as a slap to Brigham Young's operation which—by then—had succeeded in finding a home in the distant territory of Utah. It was there, far from the prying eyes of police, soldiers, and government agents that the Mormon doctrine could find its fullest and freest expression.

In 1845, the special charter of the city of Nauvoo (the one that guaranteed a certain autonomy) was revoked. In practical terms this meant that the Mormons could no longer keep a militia under arms. Sporadic attacks on Mormons by individuals and larger groups began in earnest, and Young began making preparations to leave Illinois and head west. Smith had once prophesized that their Kingdom would lay in the direction of the Rocky Mountains, so Young and his followers decided it was as good a plan as any. There was no future for Mormons in the eastern states.

After rushing to finish building the Nauvoo Temple so that followers could experience the ordinances and the endowment ceremonies, Brigham Young scheduled his exodus from Illinois in February of 1846, in deep winter and below-zero temperatures. To have waited any longer would have been suicide. Arrest warrants had been issued in December of 1845 for Young and many of the Mormon leadership on charges of counterfeiting. It seems that some of the Mormons were minting bogus coinage, referred to as "Nauvoo Bogus", and the government was using this as an excuse to level serious charges against the Mormons and close them down for good. Attempts were made by both state and federal agents to arrest Young and the others, but Nauvoo security was tight and they always managed to escape. The handwriting, however, was on the wall. Had Young waited much longer he most certainly would have wound up in prison along with most of the important Church elders. The assassinations of Joseph and Hyrum Smith while in government custody were fresh on everyone's mind. There was the additional danger that the authorities would have sent militia to Nauvoo to effect the arrests, and this could have led to a violent reaction by the Nauvoo faithful. The only option left to Young was to take as many of the Mormons with him as he could and flee not only the state of Illinois but the United States as well. He originally had planned to wait for the spring, when the weather would have been more agreable and made the traveling less arduous; however, he suddenly decided to leave in February during a harsh winter. The only logical reason for this would have been to escape the indictments and the arrest warrants, a theory that does not appear in the official Mormon websites.

So thus began what Mormons refer to as their version of the Exodus.

"We would esteem a territorial government of our own as one of the richest boons of earth, and while we appreciate the Constitution of the United States as the most precious among the nations, we feel that we had rather retreat to the deserts, islands or mountain caves than consent to be ruled by governors and judges whose hands are drenched in the blood of innocence and virtue, who delight in injustice and oppression."

 anti-Union

   Brigham Young, in a letter addressed to
   US President James Polk

The trek to Utah was anything but pleasant. The first three hundred miles took the Saints through the Iowa Territory in bitter cold weather. They made little progress, and thousands of them were scattered along the trail from Illinois to Nebraska. The last remnants of the Mormons in Nauvoo did not manage to leave until September of 1846, due to financial inability or illness, at which time mobs forced them out at gunpoint. At the end of the year, the majority of emigrants—some sixteen thousand all told—was still in Iowa while Young established his camp at Winter Quarters (now Florence), Nebraska on the Missouri River while he waited for spring and the final push to the Rocky Mountains.

  The trek was not without its internal difficulties as well. Some of the Mormons in the caravans were counterfeiters, and they were buying supplies with bogus coins. Others were bringing their coin-manufacturing equipment with them. Young, not wanting to be caught with such evidence of criminality, had the machines buried along the way. The rumor was that one day he would send teams to find the buried machines and bring them to wherever the Mormons would eventually settle so that they could begin making their own currency once again as a sovereign nation (which, in fact, they did).

  It is interesting to note the degree to which making money— literally, by minting it or printing it—was such an obsession with the Saints, beginning from Joseph Smith's early treasure-seeking days to the Kirtland Anti-Bank, and then to Utah. The association of money with Mormonism is a strong one and has not dissipated with time. It may be one example of how the alchemical concerns of the early Mormons influenced the character of the movement. Was their focus on the actual manufacture of money a manifestation of their deeper, more esoteric beliefs in the alchemical transformation?

The Catholic and Eastern Orthodox churches believe in the transubstantiaton of bread and wine into the body and blood of Jesus; the alchemists in the transmutation of lead into gold. While these ideas share some similarities—and no one can deny the wealth of the Catholic Church—the Mormons understood the spiritualization of the alchemical dream while at the same time viewing the manufacture of money pragmatically. Both the Catholic Church (for instance) and the LDS Church create wealth out of nothing: while not producing tangible goods of any value they nevertheless generate income from the "sale" of spiritual and social benefits. This could be viewed as an alchemical process reinterpreted for a lay, or non-specialized, audience. In the outer world, the LDS Church enriches itself financially, transforming the desires and anxieties buried in the hearts of their followers into treasure; in the inner, or "spirit world" of the Mormon doctrines, the individual members transform the perishable lead of their character into the gold of spiritual immortality.

In both cases—the transubstantiaton of bread and wine into the flesh and blood of Jesus, and the alchemical transformation of lead into gold—the process involves great sacrifice and the violent destruction of the original form of the *prima materia* or "first matter": the body of Jesus crucified, or the purification of the *prima materia* of the philosophers. In the case of the Mormons on their journey to the Promised Land, the sacrifices were just as severe.

By all accounts that first year on the road was a miserable one. Heavy rains had turned much of the trail to mud and long stretches became nearly impassable. Adding to the difficulties was the fact that the trip began in a hurry without adequate preparation or provisions. Along the way, Mormon settlers were stationed at various spots in Iowa to plant crops and provide housing for the emigrants who would follow.

By the spring of 1847, Young was ready to set out from Nebraska for the Great Basin in the territory of Utah. At that time, Utah was still part of Mexico and beyond the legal reach of the US government, which was what Young wanted for himself and his followers. He wanted a place that no one else wanted, reasoning that he would not have to fight other settlers or the government if he wanted to put down roots there, create his own government, issue his own currency, and practice the Mormon doctrines to their fullest degree, including polygamy. While most official Mormon and US government sources today will refer to the Mormons under Brigham Young as pioneers, they were in reality America's first expatriates. While the US Constitution guarantees a certain level of religious freedom, "religion" perhaps was too narrowly defined for the Mormons. (One has the more recent example of the flight of Jim Jones and his People's Temple congregation to the jungles of Guyana, in a move that was expressive of the same level of dissatisfaction concerning the US government as Brigham Young's. Unfortunately, a study of the parallels between Smith and Jones would require too great a digression here.)

By July 1847 the first group of Mormons entered the Great Basin, where Salt Lake City would eventually be founded, after an arduous journey through Nebraska and Wyoming. Mexico still claimed most of the territory of Texas, New Mexico and California along with Nevada, Arizona, and Utah, but there was no Mexican military or government presence in the Salt Lake City area and the 1848 war with Mexico would result in the United States winning all the land north of the Rio Grande including Utah. By that time, the first batch of Mormon settlers had already been living in Salt Lake City for a year.

Young returned from Salt Lake City to Winter Quarters, Nebraska where the largest contingent of Mormon followers still remained. On December 27, 1847 Brigham Young was named First President of the Church. In April of 1848, Young and a band of over three thousand Mormons headed for Salt Lake City to begin building the New Zion. The wagon trains that had left Nauvoo, Illinois in 1846 finally had a destination.

When Young settled in what would become Salt Lake City, his first order of business was to erect housing for his multiple wives and children. Rather than be coy about plural marriage, Young was a strong advocate. Those early days of the LDS Church saw the Saints as fiercely loyal to the doctrines handed down by Joseph Smith. They had to be: they had suffered tremendous privations and government and mob oppression due to them. They had fled across more than one thousand miles of hostile territory in wagon trains and horse-drawn carts to get to Utah, braving harsh winters, torrential rains, and sickness. To have abandoned any of the Prophet's teachings would have made all that they suffered meaningless.

So the plural marriages, the exaltations, the temple endowment and the ordinances and covenants were all still in force. The endowment would require the building of an appropriate temple, and Brigham Young's expertise as a craftsman and carpenter was put to full use in Salt Lake City as it had been in Nauvoo. His ability to lead and to organize are widely regarded as the two most important traits that his followers needed to survive the circumstances that faced them.

Other Mormons, however, were not so happy with Young's election as leader of the First Presidency. Sidney Rigdon, Joseph Smith's right-hand man for so much of the early church history, set up his own shop in Pennsylvania. Others would soon follow. Mormon splinter groups sprang up in various states, each laying claim to the Prophet's succession. The Prophet's own son— Joseph Smith III—would become head of the Reorganized Church of Jesus Christ of Latter-day Saints and his mother, Emma Harris Smith, would actually join her son's church.

Brigham Young, however, had the benefit of being recognized as the prophet's legitimate successor and as the only leader actually preserving Smith's original dream and original doctrine. He also created a new city for his followers, one that

was out of reach of government interference. This was important because Smith's doctrines involved a rejection of US government authority. By creating his own currency, his own militia,
and instituting plural marriage, Smith was setting himself and
his faithful outside the boundaries of American law and customs. He believed in creating a theocratic government, and his
run for the presidency was designed to put him in the White
House where he could overturn the Christian status quo in favor
of his own spiritual vision. He would not be a president in the
normal sense of the term; he would be a king and a prophet.

Young accepted these terms and installed himself as the king
of his new kingdom in the desert. There would be no hiding of
plural marriage: his wives and children were acknowledged and
out in the open. He created his own army. He minted his own
currency. He built his own temples, and the endowment ceremonies and anointings continued apace (the "second anointings" beginning again in 1866 after the last six hundred or so at
Nauvoo that took place by 1846). He even promulgated his own
revelations, revealing—for instance—that Adam was the father
of Jesus. And in the midst of all this frenetic activity came the
California Gold Rush.

On January 24, 1848 a discovery of gold was made at Sutter's
Mill in Coloma, California. The discoverers at first tried to keep
the discovery secret, but word leaked out to a group of Mormons
working at a nearby mill. Thus, the Mormons were among the
earliest prospectors of the Gold Rush, establishing themselves at
what would become known as Mormon Island, where they dug
for gold and in the end shipped roughly $80,000 in 1848 dol-
lars back to Brigham Young in Utah. This gold became the basis
for Young's new banking operations and helped to finance the
growth of Salt Lake City as the Mormon Mecca.

Once again, we have the image of Mormons seeking treasure
under the earth. Only this time, they succeeded. What more
validation could there be for Brigham Young's ascension to the
throne of the Mormon kingdom?

But while the situation was improving in Salt Lake City,
there were still threats from outside the kingdom. The Mexican-

American war left Utah as a territory of the United States, which meant that Young and his followers had not managed to go far enough west to avoid increasing government interference in their affairs and California would become a state in 1850, thus sealing off that potential exit. Basically, the Mormon kingdom was surrounded although that would not become apparent for some time to come.

In the meantime, Young had solidified his leadership position not only as a political and military commander but as a prophet as well. Along with the purely logistical and mundane organizing and coordinating that was so necessary to the well-being of his flock, there were also the ongoing revelations.

In Mormonism, each president of the Church is also a prophet. This is a position similar to that of the Catholic pope, who is believed to be infallible when he utters pronouncements ex cathedra. In the case of the LDS Church, the highest-ranking official takes over the title of "prophet" from his successor and is believed to have a direct line to God (or the "gods" as the case may be). Thus, Joseph Smith's legacy of—and capacity for—revelation and spiritual leadership is passed down through each successive LDS leader in an unbroken line, like apostolic succession in the Catholic and Orthodox churches. Brigham Young was the first such successor, and he flourished in the role.

It was this sense of hubris, of divine approbation, that possibly contributed to one of the church's most infamous episodes: the Mountain Meadows Massacre.

BLOOD ATONEMENT

Mormons generally hate it when the subject of the Mountain Meadows Massacre is brought up. They also hate it when polygamy, "magic underwear", and treasure-digging are brought up. That's understandable, but the historical data argues for the unconventional, antinomian nature of Mormonism especially when judged against its more mainstream Christian competitors. While one can find some justification for many of the Church's stranger deeds and doctrines, the one that cannot be excused so easily is the Massacre and its associated doctrine of blood atonement.

This was a belief that certain sins were so evil that only the spilling of the perpetrator's blood could atone for them. In other words, certain crimes were beyond even the power of the Blood of Jesus to expiate. This became a fundamental part of the Temple Endowment ritual as it was modified by Brigham Young after the murder of Joseph Smith, when the candidates were expected to take an oath to avenge his death.

Generally, the Mormons believed in capital punishment. As a Restorationist movement, they were concerned with bringing back the ancient Old Testament laws and culture, in which blood atonement and polygamy were included. Of course, Joseph Smith went far beyond the theology of the Bible when he introduced hermetic and alchemical ideas, as well as the Masonic initiation ceremonies, into his new religion along with a plurality of gods and goddesses; this was more like restoring pre-Judaic paganism than it was restoring the Law of Moses.

In the Masonic initiations that Smith adapted for his use, there were the usual "blood oaths." These are vows taken by the initiate not to reveal the secrets of the order under penalty of a violent and painful death, having one's throat cut from ear to ear. It was a small step from there to advocating blood atonement for a variety of crimes, even among the Mormon laypersons as well as non-Mormons who were considered to have sinned against the Church. This was to involve the shedding of blood— hanging or being shot was not as acceptable—and decapitation was approved as the method of capital punishment for thieves, adulterers and murderers in the Mormon kingdom until the US government extended its authority over the Utah territory.

By 1857, news had reached Salt Lake City that President Buchanan had ordered troops into Utah. The mission of these troops was not clear to the Mormons, and Young suspected that they were intended to invade the Mormon kingdom and depose Young. In response, Brigham Young declared martial law.

This was the situation in September of 1857 when a wagon train from Arkansas passed through Salt Lake City on its way to

California. These were people on their way to a better life, whole families in wagons bound for the promise of new land and new opportunities on the west coast. Salt Lake City was a regular stop for the wagon trains heading west, where they would stock up on supplies and rest before setting out for their next bivouac at Mountain Meadows in the southern part of Utah. The Baker-Fancher wagon train was no different.

While composed of mostly pioneers from Arkansas, it was rumored there were a few Missourians among them. According to the story these Missourians boasted that they possessed the actual gun that killed Joseph Smith. Of course, this rumor ignited like a lit fuse all the way back to Salt Lake City as the Baker-Fancher train made its way to Mountain Meadows. It is alleged that Brigham Young did not know in advance what was soon to take place; however, it was Young's own incendiary teachings on vengeance for the murder of Joseph Smith and the need for blood atonement that fueled this particular fire.

On September 7, 1857 a band of Mormons attacked the wagon train. What was sinister about this attack—aside from the fact that the targets were men, women and children—was the ruse used to fool the pioneers into thinking they were being attacked by Native Americans.

The Mormons had built a working relationship with the local Paiute tribes. They promised them the goods that the train was carrying if they would assist the Mormons in the slaughter. The Paiutes demurred. They had already promised not to attack white settlers and were not about to break that promise.

That meant that the Mormons would have to follow Plan B. They would dress as Indians themselves.

So for the next four days—from September 7 to September 10—the Utah Territorial Militia attacked the wagon train several times. The pioneers offered stiff resistance, but their ammunition was running low and so was their water. In order to make the destruction of the wagon train more efficient, and to solve the problem that some of the pioneers may have noticed white men among the "Indians", the Mormons decided to change it up.

On September 11, 1857 they approached the train without their Indian disguises, pretending in this case to be rescuers. They met with the leaders of the train and said that they would have to leave their belongings behind but that they would take them back to Salt Lake City to regroup.

The pioneers gratefully accepted.

The Mormons then took the adult men a little way from the women and children and executed them in cold blood.

The women were next.

Men of the militia waited in the bushes beside the road and ambushed the women and children as they passed by.

Only the youngest children (considered too young to have made good witnesses against the Mormons) were spared, seventeen in total, and these were brought back to Salt Lake City alive where they were adopted by local families until some were identified years later by government investigators and returned to their relatives in Arkansas. The property of the slaughtered pioneers was seized by the militia; some of it wound up with those few Paiutes who sided with the militia, but the rest was picked over by the militia leaders and what was not wanted by either the Paiutes or the militia was auctioned off in Salt Lake City.

Altogether more than one hundred pioneers were slaughtered at Mountain Meadows. Some estimates range as high as one-hundred-and-forty. Aside from the children, no prisoners were taken.

The leaders of the massacre made their report to Brigham Young. He issued an official statement saying that the Native Americans had been responsible for the attack. As it was in the midst of what would become known as the Utah War—the armed confrontation between Mormon militias and the US Army sent by Buchanan to suppress an alleged rebellion by the Mormons and which lasted until July 1858—an official US government investigation did not take place at once. In fact, it would be years after the end of the Civil War before anything resembling one was allowed to continue. In the meantime another massacre took place, the one known as the Aiken massacre in which six Californians were murdered.

The US Army began a preliminary investigation in 1859, after the end of the Utah War, and concluded that the Mormons had, indeed, been involved. An inspection of the Mountain Meadows site confirmed that the killings had been in the form of executions rather than the result of an Indian raid. The Army inspector was horrified by the scene—already two years' old—that confronted him of the skeletons of women with the bones of their children in their arms. He ordered that the bodies be collected and buried in a mass grave at the site, and a cross erected over it to commemorate the victims.

US officials then issued arrest warrants for the leaders of the militia, but they managed to evade capture until the start of the Civil War in 1861. Due to the war, the Mountain Meadows investigation was postponed until 1871, when authorities granted immunity to a member of the militia who gave a sworn affidavit, naming once again the Mormon ringleaders.

Although many of the perpetrators of the massacre were known, only one—John D. Lee—was ever arrested, tried and convicted of the crime. He was executed by firing squad. Brigham Young's opinion on the matter is difficult to determine precisely. Upon hearing of the massacre, he pronounced it God's judgement on the guilty. Later, in his dealings with the US government, Young began to change his story and proclaimed the massacre a "great crime". There is no indication that Young felt any guilt for his actions and statements both prior to the massacre, and later during what can only be called a cover-up. By the mid-1870s, when Lee had been executed, Young was in the midst of negotiations with the United States on the future of Utah.

Mormonism's Babylonian Exile Begins

Young had originally planned a huge nation, called Deseret, which would encompass most of the American West, down to the Rio Grande, across to California and nearly to the Canadian border. With the gradual erosion of these possibilities over time, Young was reduced to what is now the State of Utah, and had to accept American sovereignty over his "kingdom." His plans for a theocratic democracy were going by the wayside as well. The presence of US troops in the vicinity and increasing pressure from the Americans meant that he either had to risk an all-out war with the United States or arrive at some means of accommodation. The dream of Joseph Smith for a country where the Mormon ideals would be enshrined and practiced fully—a dream held dear by his successor, Brigham Young—was coming to naught. While the Mormons would continue to support plural marriage, the blood atonement, and all the other doctrinal innovations introduced by Smith and Young, they would eventually have to surrender even their most fundamental beliefs to the laws and customs of the United States, their enemy of old. These mandated changes should have provided a challenge to the constitutional amendment giving American citizens freedom of religion, but even though there was a degree of editorializing about this very issue there was no substantive dialogue about how any religion's doctrines and practices might conflict with traditional Christian ideas and thereby cause both a legal and an ethical dislocation. While the United States was not constructed as a "Christian" nation—with so many of its founding fathers committed to the ideals of the European Enlightenment, not to mention Freemasonry—the majority of its citizens considered themselves Christians and were effectively a buffer against the practice of Mormonism as well as of other, more mainstream, religious denominations such as Islam, Hinduism, etc.

The US Congress passed the Morrill Act in 1862, which outlawed plural marriage in the territories and, at the same time, removed the LDS Church incorporation charter. The Act was challenged on constitutional grounds, but was upheld in 1879 in a Supreme Court decision that stated the separation of church and state extended only to religious "belief and opinions" but not to practices. Thus, the US government arrogated to itself the right to interfere in religious ritual and the outward expression of religious belief. This is a case that has been tested at the local level many times since then, most recently concerning the practice of animal sacrifice among the believers in Latin American and Caribbean religions such as Santeria and Voudoo.

In 1890, then LDS president Willford Woodruff advised the faithful not to engage in marriages that were contrary to the law of the land. This decision did not admit of any error in church doctrine, however, but was simply a practical measure designed to reduce the tension between Utah and the LDS Church on the one hand and the US government and American public opinion on the other. This was due to the attempt by the US government to seize Church property and close down the Mormons once and for all in a law known as the Edmunds-Tucker Act of 1887 which saw many Mormon leaders go underground to avoid arrest and prosecution. In order to survive—both as individuals and as a Church—the Mormons were forced to accept legislation that went contrary to their beliefs. The Mormon manifesto banning plural marriage of 1890 was emphasized once again in another manifesto of 1904 that banned plural marriage not only in the United States and its territories, but worldwide.

With the end of (legal) plural marriage among the Mormon faithful came the end of the Second Anointing ceremony and the alchemical or "celestial" marriage that guaranteed divinity. By 1920, this ritual had been all but abandoned. The idea that one could attain divine status while alive, or obtain a guarantee that one would live in heaven after death as a god or goddess, was allowed to fade from orthodox Mormon doctrine.

By the early twentieth century, Mormonism was becoming "watered-down" and brought closer in line to American Protestantism. The emphasis on personal divinization and a multiplicity of gods (and goddesses) was downplayed in favor of language more appropriate to a Jesus-centered faith. While the Temple Endowment ceremonies continued, they remained secret and some features of mid-nineteenth century Mormonism—such as the "magic underwear" and the Masonic initiations—remained in practice. Polygamy was officially discontinued, as was the blood atonement. Religious beliefs had buckled to political expediency. Like Jerusalem to the Babylonians before it, the Mormon kingdom had become a colony of what they saw as an oppressive regime. Their temples were in danger of closing; their high priests scattered and in hiding; their assets about to be seized.

But that did nothing to hinder the spectacular growth and financial success of the Church of Jesus-Christ of Latter-day Saints far into the twentieth and twenty-first centuries. The most enduring feature of the LDS Church and of Joseph Smith's original visions would come to define the faith in the eyes of its followers as well as of its detractors. The transmutation of base materials into fabulous wealth—most of it discovered "underground"—continued at a frantic pace.

Brigham Young would die in 1877, having served as head of the LDS Church for thirty-three years. Joseph Smith himself had served as its head for only fourteen. The next fifty years would see the character of Mormonism change considerably, and when the dust settled it was obvious that if the faithful could not pile up treasures in the third, celestial heaven they would do so on the earth.

The era of the leveraged buyout had begun.

CHAPTER EIGHT

TREASURE-DIGGING IN SALT LAKE CITY

"If Joseph Smith were alive today," says a prominent Mormon businessman, "he wouldn't start a religion, he would be a leverage buyout king on Wall Street."

—Steven Naifeh and Gregory White Smith,
The Mormon Murders, p. 30

THE GRADUAL TRANSFORMATION OF THE LDS Church from a hermetically-oriented secret society to that bastion of conservative Republican politics (with the song stylings of Donny and Marie Osmond) that it is today is the result of both external pressures and internal conflicts. While the early Christians were forced underground for more than three centuries, and the Jews were hounded from one end of the earth to the other in the twenty centuries since the destruction of the Second Temple, the Mormons surrendered in less than a hundred years and assimilated to the extent that their conscience as a spiritual movement allowed.

There still were renegade groups that broke away from the main denomination and set up "fundamentalist" Mormon operations in remote areas where they could practice plural marriage, blood atonement, and all the other proscribed ordinances and covenants that had made Mormonism a household word in the nineteenth century. Some of these groups descended into nightmares of bloodshed, child molestation, and arcane rituals. Arrests of fundamentalist Mormon leaders with their plural wives occasionally make the evening news across America. Tabloid-style murder cases would shock and titillate readers with tales of crazed and introverted Mormon "fundamentalists" and their blood atonement rituals directed at religious enemies, such as the murder of Joel leBaron—the head of the Church of the Firstborn, a Mormon sect—in 1972 ordered by the leader of a rival Mormon sect.

But by far the most chilling was the case of Jeffrey Lundgren (1950–2006), the self-proclaimed prophet and former member of the Reorganized Church of Latter Day Saints (RLDS), one of the many Mormon splinter sects. He began receiving visions, and moved to a house next to the original Kirtland temple in Kirtland, Ohio: a spot sacred to the Mormons, Joseph Smith's first temple and the one he had to abandon when he fled Kirtland for Nauvoo, Illinois. Lundgren had a small group of devoted followers who believed him to be a prophet in the succession of Joseph Smith, and when he ordered them to murder an entire family of five in cold blood they complied. Lundgren had said that the father of that family—Dennis Avery—was a false prophet and had to be sacrificed. He also believed that they should seize the Kirtland Temple. After all, if Lundgren was the successor to Joseph Smith then the Temple was rightfully his.

Lundgren was eventually captured in San Diego, California a few miles from the Mexican border, was tried, convicted and executed for his crimes in 2006. His wife was sentenced to five consecutive life sentences for her role in the murders, and other members received various sentences depending on the degree to which they cooperated with the authorities.

The case had cast a strong light on the strange beliefs of the Mormons. Lundgren at one point had decided he would find the fabled "Sword of Laban" mentioned in the Book of Mormon, saying it was buried along with Joseph Smith's original golden plates. At another time, he demanded to have sexual relations with the wives of all his followers and those husbands who did not offer their spouses to Lundgren would face the same fate as the Avery family. In a way, Jeff Lundgren was Joseph Smith on angel dust.

There have been several famous serial killers who happened to be Mormons, most notably Ted Bundy and Glenn Taylor Helzer. Most recently, weird Mormon "prophets" were once again in the news with the Elizabeth Smart kidnapping case. Her captor, Brian David Mitchell, had been raised a Mormon but was eventually excommunicated from the LDS Church.

But the single most infamous of all the Mormon criminals—and the most important one for this study, since it highlights all the insecurities of the present-day LDS Church when it comes to magic, forged scriptures and treasure-digging—is Mark Hofmann.

THE SALAMANDER LETTER

It's possible that the core event of any religion determines its character for the rest of its existence in ways that are unique to that faith. If we consider the fact that the hideous torture and execution of a Jewish man in Palestine two thousand years ago is the foundational moment for Christianity, with its associated icon of that bleeding and tormented man nailed onto a cross, we may understand the Inquisition, the Crusades, and centuries of sectarian wars.

From that point of view, the association of Mormonism with forgery, the lust after gold, and the occult seems the inevitable outcome of that foundational moment in the life and career of Joseph Smith: the appearance of the Angel Moroni and a box of sacred scriptures on a hill in New York in 1823 during an act of ceremonial magic designed to discover buried treasure.

When the government forced Mormons to abandon plural marriage, the practice went underground. When the government forced Mormons to stop minting their own currency, other means were found to satisfy the craving. For decades during the twentieth century the State of Utah (and Salt Lake City in particular) was considered a major hub of investment fraud and Ponzi schemes. This was partly due to the cohesive quality of the Mormon lifestyle, in which Mormons automatically trusted other Mormons.

In 1974, the *Wall Street Journal* called Salt Lake City the "stock fraud center" of America. Ten years later, things had not improved. *Newsweek* magazine called Utah the "stock fraud capital of the nation." The publicity got so bad that the governor of the State of Utah in 1984 appointed a Securities Task Force to oversee the financial situation in an attempt to remove the stigma of fraud from the Mormon capital. Even investigative journalist Jack Anderson—himself a Mormon—got roped into one of the schemes and lost twelve thousand dollars to a Salt Lake City swindler.

In 1989, it was reported in the *Ogden Standard-Examiner* that more than ten thousand investors in the State of Utah had been fleeced of a total of over over two hundred million dollars in the previous ten years. To be fair, this was the 1980s and the era of legalized theft. Leveraged buyouts were the rage, and it was fashionable to buy up companies and loot them of their assets before firing the employees and selling off what could not be converted into ready cash.

It was also the era of the Savings and Loan crisis, in which—due to the relaxation of certain banking regulations—virtually anyone could create a "bank" under the rubric of a "savings and loan" association and obtain either a state or even a federal charter. For an investment of as little as six million dollars, one could charter a "thrift" or a "savings and loan" eligible for one hundred million dollars in federal insurance coverage. The potential for abuse is obvious. To simplify what is in reality an extremely complicated process, as the president of the thrift one could make loans to one's friends or even to oneself without any intention of repaying those loans, and then when the loans defaulted the government would cover the "losses".

While the S&L crisis is not directly related to the stock fraud situation in Utah, it demonstrates the kind of environment that was conducive to dreams of manipulating OPM: "other people's money." Gordon Gecko's mantra in the film *Wall Street*—"Greed is good"—became the slogan for a generation of investment bankers, hedge fund managers, and stock speculators. The idea was not to actually produce tangible goods, but to manipulate money in such a way that it multiplied magically without having created anything of lasting value.

To the Mormon elite this was perfectly consistent with their own doctrines. Economic success was equivalent to God's blessings, regardless of how that success was obtained. It is a peculiarly American characteristic: rather than having church members devote themselves to prayer and prosyletizing alone, there was a need for the outward trappings of religion, and these trappings had to exude the sweet smell of success. Joseph Smith needed a temple, and therefore had to find money to build one. His followers—those who came first to Kirtland and then to Illinois—were largely impoverished. He had difficulty in attracting wealthy individuals to the cause. While this was not a problem in the early days of Christianity (for instance) when devotees could meet in secret, in private homes or, later, in cemeteries and catacombs, for Joseph Smith the requirement to appear as powerful as any other mainstream denomination was paramount. This was one indication that Mormonism was not going to follow in the footsteps of New Testament religion but was instead modeled on the Old Testament model of land grabs and nation- and temple-building. It was a mundane focus that irritated many of his original flock who began to defect from Smith's brand of Mormonism—which was in constant flux with a flurry of new revelations—to the original version that was based primarily on the Book of Mormon and the story of the innocent farmboy who discovered the golden plates. Some of his early members and witnesses either left Mormonism altogether or joined one of the many splinter groups that formed both during Smith's lifetime and after. Smith began to seem as if he was suffering from delusions of grandeur and this alienated those who had stood by him in the early days.

These delusions became official Church doctrine after his death. Brigham Young was as obsessed with money and with financial strength as his Prophet, so much so that he began to see Mormonism as an economic enterprise and filled his personal coffers with Church funds. Later, after the Great Accommodation when the LDS Church was forced to surrender its most cherished principles in order to satisfy the requirements of the American government, the one principle they did not abandon was the earliest and most-formative, and most-characteristic of the early Church: treasure-digging.

Just as the money-seekers of early nineteenth century New York State were largely frauds who exploited the hopes and desperation of poor farmers with promises of buried gold and pirate booty, or the alchemical transformation of cheap coins into gold doubloons, the modern money-seekers of Salt Lake City were cast from the same mold. They promised their investors—mostly other Mormons—huge returns on their investments, and then disappeared into the desert night.

One of the more creative entrepreneurs, however, was a young man who began his career in almost the exact manner in which the pseudo-alchemists and money-diggers of 1820's New York began theirs: by counterfeiting coins. It was this initial foray into the world of bogus coins and false confidences that would eventually contribute to a major crisis among the leadership of the LDS Church in the late twentieth century.

Mark Hofmann was the product of a clandestine, early-twentieth-century Mormon plural marriage. His grandmother had been "married" in a secret ceremony, "behind a curtain" as the practice was called to keep the identities of both the man performing the marriage as well as the couple themselves a secret. His mother was a product of this polygamous marriage. It was the discovery of this fact that launched Mark on a campaign to understand what Mormonism was all about and what Mormonism valued. He felt tied to Mormonism on a social level, but alienated from it on historical and religious grounds. The core fact of his mother's questionable legitimacy would turn Mark cynical about the whole concept of "legitimacy" in general.

It began as the simple counterfeiting of American coins. As a high school student, Mark realized that the mint mark on a coin could determine its value. Some coins that were minted in a certain year in Denver might be worth more than a coin from the same year minted at a different location. So, using home electroplating equipment he would be able to change the mint mark—a tiny letter of the alphabet—from one letter to the desired one, and then sell it for much more than it was really worth.

His success at this venture emboldened him to try other types of forgery. He began to amass a collection of early Mormon memorabilia: letters, bank notes from the Kirtland Anti-Bank, old books and records, etc. He immersed himself in Mormon history, becoming a virtual expert on the subject. At the same time, he was in pre-med, studying to become a doctor. His medical plans, however, would disappear once he realized what a market there was in Mormon documents.

Especially spurious ones.

It was, in a sense, the perfect crime. Few people outside Mormonism would have known what buttons to push. Few people outside Mormonism would have had the automatic credentials that a Mormon from a good family would have. But Mark Hofmann had access to both insider knowledge, and credibility. His knowledge of early Mormon history was such that he could converse with Mormon historians with ease. He knew the type of documents that would fetch the most money, if they existed. And since he had spent so much time absorbing early Mormon literature—including diaries, letters and other written records—he could duplicate the language and even the handwriting in such a way as to fool even the most experienced document expert.

He began small, with documents purporting to be old records of Second Anointing ceremonies or secret Temple Endowment passwords and signs. He went so far as to create a forged version of the Anthon document, the one in fake Egyptian hieroglyphics that Martin Harris brought to New York City to be authenticated. He even forged a letter from Martin Harris himself!

He was able to pass all of these off as genuine documents and began to make considerable profit in the process.

Investigative journalists Steven Naifeh and Gregory White Smith have suggested that Hofmann was inspired by the novel and mini-series by Irving Wallace entitled *The Word*. The story revolves around a disaffected priest who forges a document designed to bring down the Catholic Church. If Hofmann harbored a deep antagonism against the LDS Church, then he succeeded in doing exactly what the antagonist of the Wallace novel intended, for in 1985 he landed both a virtual bombshell and a real-life bomb at the heart of the Church's leadership.

The virtual bombshell was something called "the Salamander letter." This was a letter whose contents were created entirely by Hofmann, a letter claiming to be written by Martin Harris concerning the experience of Joseph Smith on September 22, 1823 in the Palmyra forest.

Dated October 23, 1830 in Palmyra, "Harris" writes that the spirit guarding the golden plates was in the form of a "white salamander". This seems inocuous enough, considering all the other fantastic details of this episode in orthodox Mormon literature, except that the appearance of a salamander caused grave doubt to be cast on the official story.

Mormons have always been eager to disassociate occultism from the early history of the church. While much scholarship in recent years tends to support the idea that Joseph Smith and his family were engaged in various pursuits that could only be called occult by modern standards, and that the successive visits to the Hill Cumorah over the years by Smith were components of an extended occult operation involving ritual magic, the official church approach to this material is to discredit it as thoroughly as possible. They wish to characterize Smith's actions in the forest as pious attempts at prayer rather than rituals culled from Barrett's *The Magus* or any one of the other popular books on magic that were available at the time. The "Salamander letter" seemed to throw that position into serious disarray, for the entire atmosphere of the document is deeply occult. Further, the appearance of a salamander at the critical juncture of the experience would seem to indicate that dark occult forces were at work guarding the treasure rather than those of a beneficent Angel of the Lord.

Salamanders have an intriguing pedigree in European occultism. They are often associated with the element of fire— the other creatures being gnomes for earth, sylphs for air, and undines for water—and are the only one of the four elemental creatures that can be identified with an actual living animal. Salamanders also appear frequently in alchemical literature as symbols of transformation, a central focus of Mormon ritual and belief.

But there are no salamanders in the religious literature of Christianity. It is a symbol that is at best hermetic or alchemical in nature, at worst emblematic of the darkest work of the sorcerers who were reputed to make use of reptilian symbols and ingredients in their rites. The appearance of a shape-shifting salamander during Smith's first ritual in the forest was more reminiscent of Goethe's Faust meeting Mephistopheles than it was of Jacob seeing the Ladder that would take him to heaven, or Moses seeing the burning bush.

By this time, Hofmann had already sold a number of spurious Mormon documents to the leadership of the LDS Church. They had come to trust him as a valuable source, someone with connections to document collectors all over America who had access to these vital pieces of Mormon history. His income from these forgeries amounted to thousands of dollars ... each. By the time his spree had ended he had forged the handwriting and signatures of more than 120 different individuals and forged nearly 450 Mormon documents. His main goal was to create the missing 116 pages of the first transcription of the Book of Mormon, the pages that Martin Harris lost when he brought them to his wife. An audacious plan, it would have been a major coup for any forger, something on the level of the famed Hitler Diaries hoax which coincidentally was taking place the same time, in 1983, as Hofmann's first Joseph Smith forgery: a letter showing that Smith was involved in magical practices in 1825, a document that he sold to the LDS Church for fifteen thousand dollars.

But the Salamander Letter was Hofmann's crowning achievement. It was also created in 1983 and Hofmann made several attempts to sell it to the LDS Church and to other collectors of Mormon memorabilia. There were doubts about its authenticity, however, and it is also possible that Hofmann went to that particular well too many times for people began asking questions about how this young Mormon was able to source so many original documents that were critical to early Mormon history.

He finally managed to sell it to a financial manager, Steven F. Christensen, for forty thousand dollars. Christensen had intended to donate it to the LDS Church after he had it authenticated. But the doubts continued to multiply, making it difficult for Hofmann to proceed with his forging operation. He had accumulated serious debts due to a flamboyant lifestyle being financed by his forgeries and was now forced to take drastic action to cover his tracks and to divert attention away from his own misdeeds.

So in order to create a diversion he came up with a plan to deliver bombs to various individuals in the Salt Lake City area, starting with Steven Christensen.

Christensen was a bishop in the LDS Church who had been the middle-man in the donation of the Salamander Letter to the Church. He had worked for a real estate and financial services company—CFS Financial—that was going through some difficult times. The founder of CFS was his partner, Gary Sheets, who was also a bishop in the LDS Church. Sheets had taken out a life insurance policy on Christensen, which muddied the waters of what would eventually become Salt Lake City's biggest murder investigation.

For on October 15, 1985 a bomb exploded outside the sixth-floor office of Stephen Christensen in downtown Salt Lake. There had been a box propped up against the door to his office when he arrived around eight that morning. The blast killed him instantly.

No sooner had that bomb gone off than another bomb exploded in a suburb of the city, this time at the home of Gary Sheets. In this case, it was Sheets's wife Kathleen who picked up the box that was lying in the driveway of their home. She became the second fatality.

Christensen had a meeting that morning with officials of the LDS Church concerning a cache of documents that were being offered for sale by Mark Hofmann. The issue at hand was whether the documents were genuine and if the price was reasonable if they were.

In the case of Gary Sheets, his firm had gone under to the tune of millions of dollars' worth of losses to more than *three thousand* investors. That gave police a substantial list of potential suspects. But were the two bombing cases linked?

Sheets and Christensen knew each other and had been business partners. The insurance policy Sheets had on Christensen was worth five hundred thousand dollars. Thus Sheets had a financial motive for murdering Christensen. But there was no equivalent policy on his wife, Kathleen. What would have been the motive behind that attack?

It might have been the Salamander Letter.

Many Mormons were upset over the fact of the letter and the "proof" that Joseph Smith had been little more than a sorcerer when he first came into contact with the golden plates. There was every possibility that a disgruntled or angry religious zealot had decided to kill those who were involved with the Letter. As Sheets and Christensen were both bishops and business partners, and as Christensen was known to be involved with the Salamander Letter, the assumption was that the bombs were the work of those who objected to this blatant attack on their faith.

The next morning, however, things took a decidedly bizarre turn when a third bomb went off, this time in a parked car belonging to Mark Hofmann.

He had been going to a meeting with church officials: the same meeting to which Christensen had intended to go, but which had been postponed for a day so that a replacement could be found for him. The purpose of the meeting was, once again, the Hofmann documents. In this case it was a cache known as the McLellin Collection, which Hofmann claimed contained a lot of potentially explosive information on the early Mormon movement. Thus, the virtual bombshell and the real bomb met and exploded in Mark Hofmann's parked car.

Hofmann survived the blast, only to find himself eventually arrested for murder.

When the investigation was completed, it was understood that Hofmann had become worried over the impending meeting on the McLellin Collection. One of the purposes of the bomb attacks was to delay the meeting for as long as possible, as Hofmann had not had enough time to forge the documents that would be sold as the "collection." The longer he postponed the meeting, the more suspicious the church officials would become. He could not afford to have them begin questioning the provenance or authenticity of the documents he had already sold them. There were already rumors that the Salamander Letter might have been a fake. So, the purpose behind the bombs was to give everyone a legitimate reason to delay inspection of the non-existent McLellin Collection and to consider that the attacks were the plan of Mormons who took the documents very seriously and were willing to kill to suppress them. Unfortunately for him, the church decided to go ahead with the meeting anyway and examine the documents.

The third bomb was most likely designed to demolish his car with the "documents" in the trunk. This way, he could claim good faith in wanting to deliver the McLellin Collection but that the Mormon fanatics had destroyed them before he had a chance. Hofmann later claimed that the third bomb was meant for his own suicide, that once the church had decided to go forward with the meeting on the McLellin Collection that there was no way out. He owed investors more than half-a-million dollars; he owed the LDS Church about two hundred thousand dollars for a loan they had advanced to him for the McLellin Collection. He was broke, and his scheme was unraveling.

He was eventually indicted on more than twenty felony counts, including the two murders. He pled guilty, and at the time of this writing he is still in prison and will probably never get parole.

The importance of this episode to our study of Mormonism is the degree to which the LDS Church officials acknowledge their vulnerability to accusations of sorcery and "black magic." Their desperation—at the highest levels of the church—to cover up documents that could prove incriminating is an ironic commentary on a history that is anything but ordinary. The Church is sensitive to historical and archaeological research, which demonstrates that much of what appears in the Book of Mormon cannot be "true" in any generally-accepted sense of the term. They are sensitive to accusations that Joseph Smith engaged in occult practices and that these rituals—and not excessive piety—were the cause of the appearance of the Angel Moroni (if, in fact, such a vision did take place). There is a nagging suspicion among some Mormons—and a dead certainty among others—that the entire denomination is based on fraud. Mark Hofmann could not have succeeded otherwise. He would not have been able to extort—there is no other word—hundreds of thousands of dollars from Mormons for questionable documents had the LDS Church been secure in its beliefs and its identity as a mainstream "Christian" denomination.

But there was more at stake with the Salamander Letter and the McLellin Collection than simply the need to protect the Church. There was a war on, albeit a Cold War that was in its death throes, and with that Cold War there was also a culture war taking place in America. As the Gordon Geckos of Wall Street (and Salt Lake City) were telling the country that "greed is good", and as the nation went on a wild and unrestrained spree of leveraged buyouts, stock fraud, and the looting of the savings and loan associations, the rest of the world was gearing up for the impending fall of the Soviet Union and the formal defeat of Russian-style Communism, even as Chinese unrest would lead to the Tiananmen Square massacre of 1989 and the resulting consolidation of power in the hands of the Central Committee that saw China become an economic powerhouse.

But in the late 1980s, it would seem that America was living up to the promise of Joseph Smith that the New Jerusalem and the New Zion would be found—not in the Middle East of Abraham, Moses, Jesus and Mohammed, nor in the Old World of the Vatican, Martin Luther, or John Calvin—but in the New World, the world of Washington, Jefferson, Adams ... and Ronald Reagan. As the focus shifted from the Soviet Union it fell heavily on the United States: a country that had just become the world's only superpower.

The LDS President who took charge of the Mormon faithful at the time of the affair of the Salamander Letter and the Mormon Murders, and who led it during the destruction of the Berlin Wall and the dissolution of the Soviet Union, was Ezra Taft Benson.

CHAPTER NINE

HOWARD HUGHES, BOB BENNETT
AND THE MORMON SPOOKS

Two years ago when Benson was asked by an interviewer if
a good Mormon could be a liberal Democrat, he replied, "I
think it would be very hard if he was living the Gospel and
understood it."

> "Ezra Taft Benson: Will Mormons go politi-
> cal?" in *The Modesto Bee*, April 4, 1976

I think it is much easier to be a good member of the Church
and a Democrat than a good member of the Church and a
Republican."

> Senator Harry Reid, 2001

As THE 2012 PRESIDENTIAL ELECTION heated up and Mormonism became an issue—especially for Christian evangelical vot-
ers—it was not usually remarked that the Democratic Senator
from Nevada who was the majority leader of the Senate, Harry
Reid, is himself a Mormon, thus proving that Mormons can
occupy either side of the aisle. (Indeed, the first female state
senator in the history of the United States was a Democrat and
a Mormon plural wife, Martha Hughes Cannon of Utah, elected
in 1896 after defeating her own husband for the slot.) Mormonism is a minority religion in the United States, with only about
two percent of the entire population (as of 2010) professing
that faith. (Most of its membership lives outside the country in
places like Mexico and Brazil where the LDS Church is experi-
encing tremendous growth, as is evangelical Christianity in the
same areas, replacing traditional Roman Catholicism.) However,
Mormon power and influence in various areas of American society is out of proportion to its size.

As noted, Joseph Smith was the first Mormon to run for president of the United States and it was his agenda to become the chief executive and then autocratically turn the country into the Mormon version of a New Zion. His dream did not materialize, for he was assassinated before the 1844 elections took place and in any event it is doubtful that he would have secured enough votes to come in even third, much less won the presidency. But while Smith's dream did not materialize in his lifetime, it did not die with his bullet-ridden body in Carthage, Illinois.

Mormons have been involved in state and federal politics almost since the beginning of the religion. Brigham Young—Smith's successor—became governor of the State of Utah. More Mormons were elected governors, senators and congressmen over the years, and in January 2012 two Mormons were running for the Republican nomination for President, John Huntsman and Mitt Romney.

But while there are both Republican and Democrat Mormons, there is a strong perception that Mormonism equals cultural conservatism, which in turn implies political conservatism especially in the heavily-partisan landscape of late twentieth and early twenty-first century America. Mormons famously do not drink alcohol or caffeinated beverages (such as coffee or tea) and do not smoke. They are expected to be faithful to their spouses, and the Temple garments—"Mormon underwear"—are designed to maintain a state of asexuality except when the wearer is in close proximity to his or her legal significant other. Although early Mormon practices under Joseph Smith encouraged communal living and the sharing of wealth—i.e., a form of socialism—today's Mormons are expected to be staunchly anti-Communist, and to the degree that Democrats are seen as "leftist" or pro-socialist by their detractors, Mormons tend to vote for Republican candidates in national elections.

Mormons initially voted Democrat in the nineteenth century, due to their opposition to the type of conservatism represented by the Republican Party, which attacked Mormonism in 1856 because of the religion's practice of polygamy. Gradually, however, the cultural conservatism of Mormonism became allied to the political conservatism represented by the GOP and recent years have seen Mormons voting overwhelmingly Republican. More than sixty percent of Mormons voted Republican in the 1990s, for instance, compared to a national average of less than forty percent during the same time frame (the Clinton cra). But exit polls in the 2004 election showed that a whopping eighty-one percent of Mormons voted for George W. Bush. (In the hotly-contested 2000 election, *eighty-eight percent* of Mormons voted for Bush.)

Perhaps the most compelling case for the political conservatism of Mormonism in the twentieth and twenty-first centuries, however, is the prominence of a substantial number of former federal agents that comprise a security and intelligence force at the LDS Church headquarters in Salt Lake City, and which were very much involved in the affair of the Salamander Letter. This was a Mormon tradition that was inherited and maintained by the Church's most outspoken political conservative, President Ezra Taft Benson.

Benson (1899–1994) was the great-grandson of Ezra T. Benson who was a member of the Quorum of the Twelve Apostles and appointed as such by Brigham Young himself in 1846, right at the start of the exodus from Illinois. He thus had an impeccable Mormon pedigree. He did his missionary work in England from 1921-1923 before returning to the States and getting his bachelor's degree at Brigham Young University in 1926. He became heavily involved in farmers' issues, having helped found a farmer's cooperative in his native Idaho.

In 1943, Benson himself became a member of the Quorum of Twelve Apostles, and thus one of the leaders of the LDS Church. In 1953, however, President Eisenhower selected him for the post of US Secretary of Agriculture. Benson's long advocacy of farmers and farmer cooperatives made him an appropriate pick for the Cabinet position but, ironically, Benson did not agree with Eisenhower politically, believing that many of the President's economic policies smacked of socialism: a position he would maintain for the rest of his life as he flirted with extreme conservative groups such as the John Birch Society (his son became a national spokesman for the group) and with extremists such as segregationist Governor George Wallace of Alabama (Wallace had asked Benson to be his running mate in the 1968 presidential election) and fellow Mormon and former FBI agent Willard Cleon Skousen.

With Skousen (1913–2006) we arrive at an unusual destination. Skousen had been with the FBI in a largely administrative capacity (as opposed to being a field agent) from 1935–1951. A Canadian by birth to US citizens, Skousen also came from a solid Mormon background and did his missionary service in Great Britain in 1930, later obtaining a position with the Agricultural Adjustment Administration (part of FDR's New Deal program) in 1935 before joining the FBI as a clerk the same year. In 1940, he obtained his law degree and passed the bar exam in Washington, DC, becoming a Special Agent with the FBI at that time. He would eventually go on to teach at Brigham Young University and for a while served as the police chief of Salt Lake City.

The reasons are a little obscure as to why he was fired from that job in 1960. According to some sources, he had raided a poker game in which the mayor of Salt Lake City was a player ("I'm shocked, shocked! to find that gambling is going on in here." "Your winnings, sir.") According to other sources, Skousen was intent on expanding the police department budget at a time of purse-tightening, a position that put him at odds with the mayor. Whatever the reason, Skousen seems to have become embittered against authority and after his dismissal threw himself into creating the All-American Society: an ultra-right-wing organization. He also was a member of the speakers' bureau of the John Birch Society (although he never officially joined). His target was communism, and he began finding communists everywhere in society and government.

He authored a number of books on politics and on Mormon theology. His political books are well-known today due to their promotion by television personality Glenn Beck, himself a Mormon convert. Skousen's views seem to reflect a desire to "return" to the "original intent" of the founding fathers and a more pristine interpretation of the Constitution. This is perfectly in line with Mormon sensibilities, which understand the Constitution as a divinely-inspired document, tantamount to scripture. Like most scripture, of course, the interpretations of it can vary widely. In Joseph Smith's time, that meant that the Constitutional separation of church and state implied that Smith's own antinomian practices (like polygamy) should have been permitted and protected. In the twentieth century, Skousen and his followers argued for a similarly narrow interpretation while simultaneously warning everyone else that socialism and communism are rampant in the world today and most especially in the United States. Like Benson, with whom he enjoyed a long and cordial relationship, Skousen saw Eisenhower as a communist dupe and every president since Woodrow Wilson as part of a worldwide Bolshevik conspiracy, this in spite of the little-known fact that Wilson had sent an army into Russia in 1918 in an attempt to defeat the Bolshevik revolution by force.

Skousen's FBI credentials were often cited as evidence that what he wrote about was true, or at least was informed by a long career investigating communism on behalf of the Bureau. Internal FBI memos tell a different story, that of an agent who was assigned desk-duty for most of his career as an administrator and who had virtually nothing to do with security matters. The FBI eventually distanced itself from him even as J. Edgar Hoover personally blasted the John Birch Society as just as dangerous to American freedoms and security as the communists they abhorred. Skousen's repeated insistence that he was Hoover's assistant and that he was one of only two people at the FBI who could speak out against communism on behalf of the Bureau was denied in memo after FBI memo, but that didn't stop Skousen's supporters from continuing to promote these spurious relationships.

Ezra Taft Benson—who was powerful in the Church hierarchy long before he officially became president of the LDS Church in 1985—admired the FBI and included many former agents among the personnel at the Church Security office: an organization that provided security for Church officials but which also conducted surveillance and intelligence operations within the Church, even targeting prominent Mormons themselves if they appeared to deviate from Church doctrine or regulations. The leader of this group at the time of the Salamander Letter affair and appointed to the post by Benson was J. Martell Bird, a career FBI agent from 1942 to 1969 who became head of Church Security operations worldwide from 1982 until his death in 1987.

Bird had gained a certain amount of notoriety as the agent who bugged the hotel rooms of Martin Luther King in an attempt to record his dalliances with prostitutes. He also kept tabs on the anti-war movement of the 1960s, bugging the dorms of college students he felt were part of the worldwide communist conspiracy.

Bird's Church Security office was notorious among Mormons to the extent that Mark Hofmann could claim that Church Security officials had been tailing him around Salt Lake City in the hours leading up to the explosion that wounded him: a claim that had tremendous cachet among those who were familiar with how the security people operated. If the LDS Church had an "Office of the Holy Inquisition" it would be Church Security.

Another Mormon who ran interference for the Church at the time of the Salamander Letter affair was Brent Ward. The US Attorney for the State of Utah during the Reagan and George H.W. Bush administrations from 1981–1989, Ward was very close to the Quorum of the Twelve inside the Church and did what he could to insulate the Church leadership from any taint of wrongdoing in the affair of the Salamander Letter. Local law enforcement officials were frustrated in their dealings with Ward, who stonewalled the prosecution of Mark Hofmann as long as he could in order to keep Hofmann's dealings with the Quorum of the Twelve out of any legal proceedings, even going so far as to have some evidence transferred to FBI custody in order to keep it out of the hands of the police department. While Ward defended this move as necessary due to the advanced technology of the FBI laboratories, local law enforcement saw it as an effort to protect the Church at the expense of the investigation. Although Ezra Benson was not yet President of the LDS Church at the time, he and fellow member of the First Presidency, Gordon Hinckley, had taken over much of the work of the institution until Benson was installed upon the death of the ailing President Spencer W. Kimball in November of 1985 at the height of the Mark Hofmann-Salamander Letter Affair. (Ward would incidentally become a senior vice president of the Huntsman Corporation, the company founded by the father of Jon Huntsman Jr., the Mormon candidate who ran unsuccessfully against fellow Mormon Mitt Romney in the 2012 Republican presidential primaries. Ward was also an outspoken critic of pornography and led a well-publicized campaign against smut for many years.)

Benson, like his colleague Skousen, was a Cold War ideologue. Communism was the "terrorism" of the 1950s through 1980s, until the fall of the Soviet Union. Both Benson and Skousen (and Martell Bird) saw Communists everywhere, at every level of society. As noted in many other places—such as in Arthur Miller's famous play, *The Crucible*—it was a mindset similar to the Catholic Church's fear of witchcraft during the Middle Ages, or Mormonism's own suspicion of "secret combinations. " While Communists certainly did—and do—exist, the powers ascribed to them by true believers such as Benson and Skousen bordered on the supernatural. It was the beginning of the phenomenon of the modern conspiracy theorist.

Paranoia is a hallmark of conspiracy theory, popularly understood. It is possible that paranoia has taken a bad rap of late for, as the *New York Times* literary critic, Anatole Broyard, once remarked, "Paranoids are the only ones who notice anything anymore." A healthy inclination towards suspicion is necessary to the development of conspiracy theories; if one accepted the view of the world as presented by media outlets, government pamphlets, or ministers of religion then one could live blissfully in the present only, until such time in the future as war breaks out, or the economy collapses, or when most needed, divine intervention fails to take place.

The incredible destructive power of the atomic bomb did not manufacture paranoia or suspicion, but it did consolidate them. Humans had taken upon themselves the potency of gods; not since Biblical times (Sodom and Gomorrah, or the Flood) had so much devastation been wrought—twice—on the planet. As long as the powers-that-be were as mortal as we were, and as vulnerable to a sword point or a gunshot, we could complain about them or take arms against them; but with the advent of atomic weaponry that suddenly was not possible. Warfare had been taken out of the hands of the individual soldier and made into an instrument of corporate entities. We lived on the edge of an abyss of sudden annihilation, and this—more than any other single factor, in my view—contributed to the paranoia about secret societies controlling the destinies of the world. After all, no one knew the atomic bomb existed until August of 1945. Its development had been America's best-kept secret for years. What other secrets were there? What other possible sources of devastation and control were under wraps?

And when the Soviets began testing their own atomic weapons it seemed as if the fears of the paranoid had come true with a vengeance. There was some other cabal, some secret group, that controlled the flow of technology and which was above and beyond all notions of national borders and ideological boundaries. As the Cold War became progressively desperate, men like Robert Welch, the founder of the John Birch Society and friend of both Skousen and Benson, began to write of the Illuminati.

The problem with paranoia is that it is open-ended. There will always be one more level of conspiracy, one further step to take to uncover the real enemy. Paranoia becomes a kind of religion, where faith in a divine ruler is replaced by fear of a satanic power. Love of God is transformed into horror of the Anti-

Christ. The Bavarian Illuminati is the icon of this type of conspiracy theory, the umbrella organization for everything from the various American political parties to the Ford Foundation, the Rockefellers, the Council on Foreign Relations, the Trilateral Commission, and the Bilderbergers, not to mention the Socialists, the Communists, the Fascists and the Nazis.

Admittedly, the US government did not do much to ameliorate the situation. When it was bruited about that there were as many undercover FBI agents in the Ku Klux Klan as there were genuine members, for instance, the take-away was that the existence or threat of radical extremism was a myth perpetrated by spin-doctors in government-sponsored think tanks. Secrecy and deception are the twin pillars at the entrance to the Temple of Paranoia and, after all, "if you're not paranoid you don't have all the facts."

Joseph Smith was paranoid, as most successful leaders are. He was being hunted by a variety of government agents, the military, and local citizens who objected to his lifestyle and his politics as well as his religion. At first he condemned secret societies, and then later he embraced Freemasonry. He had multiple wives, which fact he tried—with various levels of success—to keep from his legal wife, Emma Harris. He believed that the Bible as commonly understood was in error, that there were three gods present at the creation and that humans could become gods (thus supporting the claim of the Serpent in the Garden of Eden). He institutionalized secrecy in the LDS Church, particularly in the form of the Endowment ceremonies. This view of the world as being comprised of secret powers, secret names, secret handshakes and secret knowledge, as well as secret spouses— and of the persecution of the LDS Church at the hands of the US government—is a view that is reflected in the work of the intelligence agencies who spy, and who conversely are fearful of spying. The bomb—and the associated Cold War that had as much to do with its destructive potential as it did with ideology—raised these stakes to an incredible level. Men like Benson and Skousen are products of this complex environment: a world in which the political and military reality of the Cold War is combined with the occultism and antinomian beliefs and practices of the LDS Church.

But Mormon politicians and Mormon theologians are the tip of an iceberg whose bulk lies below the surface of American politics. In those frigid depths a number of loose ends in American culture are frozen together in that shadowy world where private security services and covert intelligence operations meet.

To illustrate this we can begin with the story of one of America's richest and most controversial tycoons, the colorful hermit whose last years (and death) remain cloaked in mystery to this day, and whose fear of the government, of the atomic bomb and of atomic testing, caused him to surround himself with a Mormon bodyguard, a group of men who, it could be assumed, shared his view that the powers-that-be were up to no good.

Howard Hughes.

As many people know, Hughes was an inventor, a test pilot, an engineer, and a movie producer. For much of his life he was a celebrity who squired some of the most beautiful women in Hollywood. But in his last years he became a recluse, fearful of germs and afraid of spies.

Like many corporate tycoons, he liked to employ former FBI agents. They have a reputation for honesty and courage, and for loyalty. But unlike other tycoons, he also liked to hire Mormons.

Pious Mormons famously do not drink or smoke. They cultivate a conservative lifestyle. The white shirts and dark suits of the Mormon missionary inadvertently mimic the outfit of the traditional FBI agent. Both are respectful to authority, and both respect the need for secrecy when required. While Hoover was alive, it would have been difficult to tell a Mormon from a Special Agent, except perhaps for the gun and even then, not necessarily.

But Mormons are answerable to God; the FBI agent is answerable to the US government, even after retirement when the agent is expected to keep the Bureau's secrets to himself. Hughes had a former FBI agent on staff, the inimitable Bob Maheu (1917–2008). Maheu had worked not only as an FBI agent but also had the CIA as a client, most especially during the time when the US government attempted to assassinate Fidel Castro of Cuba.

But Maheu, a Democrat and close friend of both John F. Kennedy and Robert F. Kennedy, was eventually fired from the Hughes operation after more than a decade of working for it. He lost the battle to Frank William "Bill" Gay, a Mormon who was the man credited for having formed the "Mormon Mafia" at the Hughes empire. The Mormon Mafia was a group of six who formed an impenetrable phalanx around Hughes, thus effectively taking control of his empire. No one could see Hughes; no one could communicate with Hughes except indirectly through the "Mafia." For the head of one of America's most important defense contractors with the highest level security clearances, this was an absurd—if not exceedingly dangerous—state of affairs. It meant that the Mormon bodyguard, under the command of Bill Gay, was running the Hughes empire under the umbrella organization known as the Summa Corporation (which critics cynically said stood for "Southern Utah Mormon Missionary Association").

To make matters more interesting, the doctor who was supplying a constant flow of drugs to Hughes—who had become increasingly dependent on Valium, codeine, and other pharmaceuticals—was another Mormon, Dr. Wilbur Thain, Bill Gay's brother-in-law. As Hughes began failing and frantic phone calls were made to Thain to fly down to Mexico and look after his patient, Thain postponed his trip for several days and had to be hunted down and virtually forced onto a plane. When he finally arrived at the Hughes suite in Acapulco, he spent several hours shredding documents. No one seems to know what documents they were, or why they had to be shredded, and why Thain had to do (or was allowed to do) the shredding. It might have had something to do with the over five thousand prescriptions Thain had written for Hughes over a four year period. Thain—like Adolf Hitler's personal physician, the quack Dr. Morrell—kept his patient going with excessive medication, some of it injected intravenously and some of it in pill form.

According to research by author Geoff Schumacher in *Howard Hughes: Power, Paranoia and Palace Intrigue,* Bill Gay and the Mormon Mafia had been adjusting Hughes's medication in order to control his moods and therefore his decision-making. When Gay decided that it was time to get rid of Maheu, Hughes was manipulated into giving the order. The Hughes estate itself, via a legal memorandum filed in 1980 concurred in this characterization of the Mormon Mafia when it came to exercising control over the Old Man. Maheu himself, in an interview given in 2007 (the year before he died) agreed that this is how the scenario played out, with the Mormons effectively taking complete control of Summa Corp by drugging its founder.

That the CIA had a special relationship with the Hughes organization during the last years of Hughes's life when he was in the effective control of the Mormon "Mafia" can be seen in the celebrated episode of the Glomar Explorer. This was a deep-sea drilling vessel that was commissioned by the CIA to serve in the recovery of a sunken Soviet submarine in 1974, a mission that was at least partially successful. The cover story was that the Glomar Explorer was drilling for manganese on the ocean floor, but this legend was exploded shortly after the recovery of the sub. What is not known for certain is the degree to which Howard Hughes himself was consciously aware of the project, or of his organization's close ties to the American intelligence community.

Now, at the Princess Hotel in Acapulco, Mexico in 1976, the days of controlling Hughes were coming to an end. Panicked, the Mormon guards demanded that Thain come immediately to Mexico to revive the man whose wealth and power had ensured their extravagant lifestyles and substantial bank accounts. Hughes's abhorrence of the atomic testing taking place in the Nevada desert had driven him out of the country altogether; well, that and the numerous subpoenas that were floating around demanding his physical presence in one courtroom or another, something which the Mormon Mafia could not contemplate since as soon as Howard Hughes showed up in his flowing hair, his long uncut fingernails, and overall filthy and unbathed condition, the jig would be, as they say, up. It could have been argued that the mental state of Howard Hughes was a national security matter, since he controlled a vast empire of defense-related technology and manufacturing, but that was the point: he didn't control it. Bill Gay did. And Bill Gay's brother-in-law was seconded to the project of keeping Hughes tame and generally stoned.

One of the projects undertaken by Gay during the few years immediately before Hughes's death was a planned break-in at the office of Republican Hank Greenspun, (1909–1989), the rambunctious editor of the Las Vegas *Sun*. Greenspun had been instrumental in helping Hughes buy the Desert Inn in Las Vegas and in other business dealings in the state. It was believed that Greenspun's office safe had documents which would be incriminating to Democratic presidential candidate Ed Muskie, and James W. McCord—one of the Watergate "Plumbers"—admitted that plans were made to break into Greenspun's office and steal the documents for later use by then President Richard Nixon in his 1972 campaign for re-election. However, many others believe that these documents were in actuality evidence of business dealings between Howard Hughes and Bebe Rebozo, Richard Nixon's longtime friend and "fixer," which, if revealed, would hurt Nixon's re-election chances. Regardless, the documents from Greenspun's safe never saw the light of day as the crusading editor managed to squash an attempt by the Watergate committee chaired by Sam Ervin to obtain them for their investigation into criminal wrongdoing by Nixon and the Plumbers.

But the Mormon connection to Watergate went even further than this. Mormon politician Robert Bennett had a role to play that was more deeply on the covert side of the scandal and which involved some of the most famous players in the affair, including former CIA Bay of Pigs action officer and Watergate Plumber E. Howard Hunt.

Robert Bennett (born in 1933) is the son of the late Senator Wallace Foster Bennett (1898–1993), the head of a family with an excellent Mormon pedigree, as the Bennetts were related by marriage to Heber J. Grant, the seventh president of the LDS Church and one of its most famous leaders. Robert Bennett served as a Mormon chaplain with the Utah Army National Guard for twelve years before becoming the president and owner of the Robert Mullen Company in 1971.

The Robert Mullen Company was a public relations firm that had been founded in 1952 by Robert R. Mullen, a press secretary for Dwight Eisenhower in the 1952 presidential campaign. Mullen did a lot of work for the LDS Church in the public relations arena, including introducing the Mormon Tabernacle Choir to audiences in Europe and writing a pro-Mormon propaganda book, *The Latter-day Saints: The Mormons Yesterday and Today.* Mullen also worked for the Nixon-Agnew presidential campaign in 1968 and, as the Howard Baker Watergate Report affirmed (and was reported in *Newsweek* in 1974), Mullen's company had been providing cover for CIA employees from 1959 to 1972. When Mullen retired from the firm his former Nixon campaign employee Bennett took it over and brought Hughes's Summa Corporation in as one of its clients. This was at the same time that E. Howard Hunt became an employee of Mullen, using the PR firm as a cover for his other activities.

That Mullen was used as a CIA front is common knowledge today, due to the revelations made during the Watergate investigations. The author had been personally acquainted with the agent—a colleague of Hunt—who was sent to Singapore under Mullen cover, and who debriefed Chinese defectors there. (In recent years, I tried to obtain incorporation information from the Singaporean Companies House on the Mullen Company operation in that country, but was met with stiff resistance even though the operation closed down about thirty-five years ago.)

That there was close cooperation between the Mullen Company and the CIA as well as the LDS Church has been well-documented. Bennett's administration of the company came at a time when Cold War tensions were high, the Vietnam War was still in full swing, and the Glomar Explorer operation was up and running. The Hughes-Mormon-CIA nexus was as tight as ever. It remains a matter for later historians to decide whether or not the Hughes empire would have been as amenable to CIA operations as it was if the "Mormon Mafia" was not the de facto ruling elite of the corporation. With Bennett in charge of the Mullen front company in Washington DC, and Bill Gay in charge in Las Vegas with Summa Corporation, we have a fascinating glimpse into the way the world worked in the 1970s. Mormons, because of their sobriety, cultural and political conservatism, and respect for authority, became entrusted with some of the deepest secrets of the American intelligence community. Some also enabled the Watergate Plumbers in their mission of playing "dirty tricks" on their political opponents. One of these— a student from Brigham Young University, Thomas Gregory— worked directly with E. Howard Hunt, Gordon Liddy and the other Plumbers in collecting information from the Muskie and McGovern campaigns while posing as a volunteer. This young man quit the Plumbers only days before the famous Watergate break-in and thus managed not to become embroiled in that scandal. In fact, as the Senate Watergate Report demonstrates, the actual planning of the Watergate break-in took place at the Mullen Company offices at 1700 Pennsylvania Avenue, a location conveniently across the street from Nixon's Committee to Re-Elect the President (otherwise known as CREEP) at 1701 Pennsylvania Avenue where Watergate co-defendant, G. Gordon Liddy, had his office.

Further, as the Watergate documentation demonstrates, Robert Bennett himself had a CIA case officer to whom he reported, thus showing that the Mullen Company was a creature of the Agency as well as of the Hughes empire, and was the propaganda arm of the LDS Church from whom Hunt would source suitable covert operatives in his quest to undermine the democratic process.

To be sure, not all Mormons were, or are, fanatic anti-communists, or spies, or even registered Republicans. There have been, and continue to be, many Mormons who are members of the Democratic Party (such as Sen. Harry Reid) and many who have been staunch supporters of ethical political activism on both sides of the aisle. There have been many prominent Mormon Republicans who were and are moderates, such as Michigan Governor George Romney (1907–1995), the father of Mitt Romney, who ran an unsuccessful campaign for the presidential nomination in 1968 and who wound up as Nixon's Secretary of Housing and Urban Development.[7] A fair politician and former head of American Motors who disagreed with Nixon on many issues—from the Vietnam War to housing for the poor—he left the administration at the start of Nixon's second term and went into private life. His cousin Marion Romney (1897–1988) was also born in Mexico and eventually became a member of the First Presidency of the LDS Church alongside Ezra Taft Benson and Gordon Hinkley.

The close cooperation of important church personalities such as Bill Gay, Robert Bennett and others with the Hughes empire, the CIA, and the Watergate affair, indicates that a certain mindset existed within the Mormon community that saw the end justifying the means. It also implies a close cooperation that existed between the LDS Church and American intelligence operations, at least during the heady days of the Cold War if not later. Robert Bennett provided cover for CIA agents E. Howard Hunt and Arthur Hochberg, and others whose names and functions we do not know and probably will never know. Hunt interfaced with the Hughes empire via Bennett on several projects at the time when the Hughes-CIA cooperation was at its height … at a time when Hughes himself was being manipulated by the so-called "Mormon Mafia."

But that was then. This is now.

---

7 George Romney was born in the state of Chihuahua in Mexico, to American parents, and this fact has given rise to statements by Mitt Romney that he is the "son of Mexican immigrants." The Mormon family was forced to leave Mexico at the start of the 1910 Revolution whose targets included Mormon colonies.

Robert C. Gay—the son of Bill Gay, Hughes executive and leader of the "Mormon Mafia"—is not a well-known name to many Americans, but he is currently CEO and co-founder of Huntsman Gay Global Capital, a private equity firm with offices in California, Florida, Massachusetts and Utah. According to the Huntsman Gay website, "Huntsman Gay Global Capital is a $1.1 billion private equity fund focusing on leveraged buyout, recapitalizations and growth equity transactions in the middle market." It numbers among its directors Jon Huntsman (father of Jon Huntsman Jr., the erstwhile GOP candidate for president) as well as Gregory Benson, who previously had worked for a company known as Bain Capital. Prior to Huntsman Gay, however, Robert Gay was managing director for Bain Capital, working alongside his friend and colleague Mitt Romney for sixteen years.

Business journalists have targeted Bain Capital as an example of the type of leveraged buyout strategy that characterized the 1980s and 1990s. In an article by Michael Barbaro in the New York *Times* of November 12, 2011 a test case cited is that of Dade International, a medical device manufacturer located in Illinois. Romney, who created Bain Capital, managed to double Dade International's sales. At the same time, however, Bain also quadrupled its debt. Nearly 1,700 employees lost their jobs by the time Bain was finished with the company and it filed for bankruptcy protection.

This is how it worked: in 1994 Bain invested in Dade by borrowing $450 million from investors, including Goldman Sachs, and only investing $30 million of its own funds to buy the company. This strategy limited Bain's own risk and there is nothing illegal or unethical about that. Bain would then force the company to make acquisitions, buying up competitors left and right. At first, it seemed to be working.

Dade's annual sales doubled; its assets tripled ... and its debt nearly tripled, to a whopping $816 million by 1998 from $298 million in 1994.

Romney's strategy was to force Dade to buy back its shares in Bain Capital, which it could do only by borrowing more money.

Bain Capital and its investors got $353 million from the deal, while some Dade executives walked away with $55 million. But Dade began cutting more jobs, owing creditors almost $2 billion and finally filing for bankruptcy in 2002.

However, after it emerged from bankruptcy protection Dade found itself bought by the German firm Siemens for $7 billion in 2007. While those who were executives at Dade thought that, overall, the experience with Bain Capital had been positive notwithstanding the bankruptcy, the actual employees of Dade thought otherwise, of course.

I bring this up not to besmirch either Bain Capital or Mitt Romney. As someone who has worked for multinational corporations and as an executive with two American manufacturers, I am not naive in the way the world works. While I don't agree with the leveraged buyout technique of using companies as cash cows or ATM machines at the expense of their employees, I realize that it is nevertheless legal and part of doing business worldwide.

Which, admittedly, may be part of the problem.

The point I am trying to make is somewhat different. Joseph Smith began his career as someone trying to locate buried treasure. This treasure was buried either by Native Americans, or by pirates, or by some other individuals. Regardless, it still was "other people's money." Whether it had been gained by piracy, or buried by people who had earned it honestly, Smith's focus—and the focus of all those who were similarly engaged in treasure-digging pursuits at the time—was to discover hidden wealth. Wealth that had been created by someone else.

Smith's family was suffering through difficult economic times. Wealth was a dream, a seduction. There seemed to be no way to make money "the old-fashioned way"—i.e., to earn it—so the only alternative was to steal, or to find someone else's lost and abandoned earnings. I am not blaming the seventeen-year-old Smith for doing his best with bell, book and candle to locate money or valuables that would rescue his family from poverty. But the attitude that is nurtured through this occupation is questionable, at best. Bain Capital saw in Dade—and in more than one hundred other companies—a source of buried treasure. The techniques they used implied a higher respect for lucre than for labor. This is not a problem that is unique to the financial "wizards"—I use the term advisedly!—or to Mormons, but to an American preoccupation with material wealth that may be due more to some kind of Calvinism run amok than to capitalism the way it is normally understood, or practiced. But with Bain Capital in the 1990s—as with Salt Lake City generally in the 1980s—the Mormon focus on obtaining wealth through almost "magical" means was everywhere in evidence.

It was not for nothing that Joseph Smith was called "the first leveraged buyout king".

That being said, what are the implications for a "Mormon presidency"?

IMPLICATIONS

CHAPTER TEN

IMPLICATIONS

Believing with you that religion is a matter which lies solely between Man & his God, that he owes account to none other for his faith or his worship, that the legitimate powers of government reach actions only, & not opinions, I contemplate with sovereign reverence that act of the whole American people which declared that their legislature should "make no law respecting an establishment of religion, or prohibiting the free exercise thereof", thus building a wall of separation between Church & State.

Thomas Jefferson, 1802

I believe in an America where the separation of church and state is absolute—where no Catholic prelate would tell the President (should he be Catholic) how to act, and no Protestant minister would tell his parishoners for whom to vote— where no church or church school is granted any public funds or political preference—and where no man is denied public office merely because his religion differs from the President who might appoint him or the people who might elect him. I believe in an America that is officially neither Catholic, Protestant nor Jewish—where no public official either requests or accepts instructions on public policy from the Pope, the National Council of Churches or any other ecclesiastical source—where no religious body seeks to impose its will directly or indirectly upon the general populace or the public acts of its officials—and where religious liberty is so indivisible that an act against one church is treated as an act against all.

John F. Kennedy, 1960

I have written about Mormonism previously and have been fascinated by the religion for reasons having nothing to do with politics. The history of the LDS Church and most especially of its founder and prophet, Joseph Smith Jr., is a treasure-trove of occultism, hermetic beliefs, early Americana, and the Old West. It is, as Mitt Romney has declared, an "American religion", as "American as apple pie." You will get no objection to that from me.

But America is a complex country with a complicated and deeply-textured history. The plight of those fleeing religious persecution in Europe became mixed with the inhuman crime of slavery. Religious sectarianism and political rivalry became the breeding ground for witchcraft accusations and charges of heresy. The persecution of the Native American population took place at the same time that America was fighting wars of independence, conquest, and the Civil War. The nation has gone through many periods of economic boom and bust, many depressions, much civil unrest.

America has a Constitution of which it rightfully can be proud, yet there is no agreement as to what it really means. This is particularly the case when it comes to the famous "separation of church and state," a phrase that is found nowhere in the Constitution itself but which finds its expression in the First Amendment to the Constitution which states "Congress shall make no law respecting an establishment of religion, or prohibiting the free exercise thereof."

This "wall of separation" as Jefferson called it is a purely legal concept. Obviously, government officials, employees and politicians running for office have religious convictions—or lack of convictions—that they either express or conceal. It is the degree to which these convictions may influence political action that concerns us here. The degree to which a religious conviction is sincerely held is also a measure of a politician's character.

America has often been called a "Christian country," but that is mostly wishful thinking on behalf of Christians. The Founders were nominally Christian for the most part, but there can be no denying that Enlightenment ideals were part of the motivation for the separation of America and England in the eighteenth century. As most of us are aware, many of the Founders were Freemasons, men who believed in a One God and yet who were not sectarian in their outlook but rather respected all religions. If America was intended to be a Christian country that concept would have been enshrined in the Constitution. It was not. Instead, the First Amendment makes it clear that there would be no attempt by the US government to impose any specific religious belief on the people.

That statement would be sorely tested many times over the course of American history. One such test was the practice of polygamy. The government decided that polygamy was illegal and did not have the protection of the Constitution regardless of whether or not it impacted the religious beliefs of the Mormons. The view was that the freedom of religion enshrined in the Constitution referred to beliefs and not to actions, i.e., that the government could not tell you what to believe but it could tell you how to behave. This is an echo of the statement by Jefferson, above, in a letter to a Baptist community in Danbury, Connecticut, that the "legitimate powers of government reach actions only ... ".

Thus, one can believe in polygamy but not practice it.

The Great Accommodation—as it was called—by the LDS Church to accept this ruling and outlaw polygamy among its followers was a step towards acknowledging the supremacy of the American Constitution over the revelations of the prophet, Joseph Smith. To be sure, Mormons believe that the Constitution is a kind of scripture and hold it in deep reverence. But what this has done is create a kind of religious and political paradox: it has made of Mormonism a truly "American" faith, more than any other. Does this mean that spiritual or religious convictions are identical to political beliefs, at least among the Mormons?

Jack Kennedy, when running for president in 1960, was forced to defend his membership in the Roman Catholic Church at a time when opponents believed that having a Catholic president meant that the Pope would have control over America's government. Unique among major religions, Mormonism can claim that there is no foreign power that has any influence whatsoever over its organization, its doctrine, or its people. There is no foreign Pope, no Archbishop of Canterbury, no Grand Mufti to contend with; no Rome, no Jerusalem, no Mecca. While it acknowledges the importance of the King James Bible, it has its own scripture—the Book of Mormon—written in America and discovered by an American, which is concerned with (an admittedly spurious) American history. It has its own Vatican, in Salt Lake City. It has its own priesthood, and its own American Prophet.

And it has accepted the American Constitution as over-ruling its revelations.

This begs us to ask the question which is at the heart of the First Amendment statement concerning government and religion, but which is a question that has never been asked (to my knowledge). If government "can make no law respecting an establishment of religion", what if a religion makes a law respecting an establishment of government? What if a religion—any religion—relinquishes its beliefs and practices to be more in line with government beliefs and practices? This may sound absurd, but it is exactly what happened with the LDS Church, and the implications are serious.

While the US government did not create a religion, a religion has aligned itself with what it perceives to be government doctrine and actions to the extent that one could be forgiven for wondering if such a church can be an extension of government policy. And since we have an adversarial political situation in the United States, which gets more partisan by the day, one then is forced to wonder if such a church will then take sides with what it believes to be the "true government."

While rank and file Mormons cover the entire spectrum of American political membership—and while many previous Mormon leaders have been outspoken on both sides of the Congressional aisle as well as at Church headquarters—the polarization that has taken place in America since the Cold War years makes us wonder if the LDS Church (or a powerful cabal within the Church) has a political agenda. That there was such a cabal and such an agenda in the 1970s and 1980s is obvious from the public record. Mormons as Mormons were significant players at the highest levels of the Nixon administration, for instance, with the involvement of the Mullen Company and Robert Bennett in the Watergate affair. And the voting statistics for Mormons in the past three or four election cycles demonstrates their overwhelming support for GOP candidates, outvoting even evangelical Christians in the election, for instance, of George W. Bush.

The causus belli of the Missouri War against the Mormons began with the perception that Mormons voted as a bloc. Missourians attempted to prevent Mormons by force from entering the voting booth due to this perception. While it may be a myth that the entire membership of any religion votes as a bloc, there is sufficient evidence to show that religion does matter when it comes to elections. It was an issue for Jack Kennedy; and when he successfully answered the Catholic question and squeaked to a narrow victory over Richard Nixon in 1960, he was charged instead with being "soft on Communism" and a traitor to the country. It was an issue for George W. Bush, who famously claimed that he was answering a divine call to become president. It became an issue for Barack Obama, who many claimed was either a closet Muslim or allied with anti-American sentiments voiced by the Protestant minister Rev. Wright.

Religion may once again become an issue in the 2012 election, and in succeeding elections. If Mitt Romney becomes the Republican nominee, Mormonism will become an issue. If Rick Santorum had become the nominee, Roman Catholicism would have once again become an issue. As of this writing, it appears that evangelical Christians—who turned out strongly for Bush in 2000—are supporting Santorum, the Catholic, against Romney. This is truly a strange state of affairs, for many evangelicals have considered Roman Catholicism—"Popery"—to be one step removed from Satanism. But at least Roman Catholics are demonstrably Christian. The same cannot be said—by evangelical Christians—for Mormonism.

The LDS Church has tried, with varying degrees of success, to distance itself from some of the more contentious views of its founders and to portray itself as mainstream Christian. As anyone who has read the preceding chapters will swiftly realize, Joseph Smith's form of Christianity was closer to Gnosticism than the Gospels. There are many points of departure between Mormonism and Christianity, from a plurality of gods to the divinization of human beings, to post-mortem baptisms of unwitting dead people, to secret Temple ceremonies involving passwords and handshakes, to the famous "Mormon underwear". While polygamy has been officially prohibited by the LDS Church, it persists underground and in the popular culture as television series such as HBO's *Big Love* demonstrate.

What, then, are the implications for a Mormon presidency?

On social issues, the LDS Church has come out against gay marriage, for instance. It resisted allowing African-Americans full membership until the late twentieth century, due to the belief that they had been "cursed" by their black skin. The LDS Church has been culturally conservative for nearly one hundred years, and reflects many of the mores of what is usually—disparagingly—called "middle America," with all of the (generally unfair) allegations of racism, sexism, and homophobia that the term implies. These are the characteristics that are generally known.

What is not a matter of public discourse, however, are the secret beliefs and practices that may influence a candidate's actions. When George W. Bush and John Kerry were asked, for instance, about their membership in Skull & Bones—the famous secret society with its headquarters at Yale University—neither gentleman felt it was incumbent upon them to respond to the question since they had taken oaths of secrecy to the Order. For a candidate for President of the United States, this evasion should be unacceptable. This was not a First Amendment issue, for Skull & Bones is not a religion, nor were beliefs being questioned, only actions. But the questions remained unanswered.

There are also secret ceremonies at the Temple. Polygamy, while prohibited by the LDS Church, is still a Church doctrine. So is exaltation, or divinization. Celestial marriage. Baptism of the dead. The maintenance of huge genealogical and now genetic databases at the Temple in Salt Lake City. There has been an invasion of privacy by the LDS Church in a very unusual and unsettling way; it is entirely possible that my own ancestors have been baptized by proxy in some obscure rite in some distant Temple and while I may not believe in the concept of proxy baptism, nor believe that the Mormons are actually capable of causing spiritual changes to occur in the souls of dead people, I am nonetheless disturbed by the calm insistence of a powerful and wealthy denomination that they have the right to do so, and to people who are genetically and genealogically connected to me.

And, one day, long after I have shuffled off this mortal coil, there may be some well-meaning but otherwise clueless Mormon who will stand in for my soul and pronounce me baptized in this most American of American religions.

Will a Mormon president change America in any appreciable way? It is hard to imagine that this would be the case, but that may be the secret to Mormon success in business as well as in politics. The Church has had to disguise itself for so long—to conceal its strange and striking doctrines from all but the most devoted scholars and paranoid conspiracy theorists—that dissembling has become second-nature. They wear the secrets of their religion the way they wear their Temple garments: under their street clothes, invisible to the naked eye, and never to be removed. Mormons in general benefit by being considered boring and traditional, when they are anything but.

Scientology had its origins in the same arcane beliefs and practices as Mormonism. L. Ron Hubbard began his "religious" career as a partner of Aleister Crowley-devotee Jack Parsons. Together, these two magicians used the rituals set down by the same sorcerers as those who inspired Joseph Smith: Agrippa, Solomon, Moses, Francis Barrett. Hubbard, like Smith, saw angels in the American wilderness, summoned by ceremonial magic. Scientology, too, is a quintessentially "American" religion, dedicated to the pursuit of wealth and political power.

But while Mormonism is boring and traditional, Scientology is weird and controversial. One could say that Scientology may be closer to the antinomian practices of magic than Mormonism seems to be, but that might be a serious error of judgment.

Did Joseph Smith really see golden plates on which were written the scriptures of his faith? Before we answer that question, we have to ask another one.

Did Moses really see God write the Ten Commandments on stone tablets? Did Moses even really exist as an identifiable human being?

Or did Jesus really rise from the tomb?

Wasn't Joseph Smith a real prophet in the line of Moses, if by prophet we mean someone who created a religion and fabricated a scripture in order to shout down the pragmatists, the realists, the atheists, and those who had lost their faith along with their wealth and status? Wasn't Joseph Smith, in trying to give himself and his impoverished family some hope, some belief in a better future, also encouraging others to see America as he saw it: a wild land populated by the descendants of the Lost Tribes, a New Zion for the world to replace the one lost in Palestine? A land of tremendous promise and potential?

If a Mormon becomes president, will he sincerely believe in Mormonism? And, if so—or if not—would that be a good thing or a disaster for America?

That would depend, of course, on your own understanding of what it means to be an American. Which is based, of course, on what you believe America to be. And on how you view your own religion, and on how important its core beliefs—its credo— is to you and your life.

And how you see your religion and the American experiment working together, or working apart.

The question of a Mormon presidency is oddly removed from Republican or Democrat allegiances. As we have noted, Mormons can be found in both political camps like members of Skull & Bones, or Freemasons. Thus it is not the purpose of this book to attack Mormonism, but to reveal it ... just the way I have written about Freemasons and secret societies in my other works. At the present time, however, it would appear that mainstream Mormonism and the GOP have become somewhat allied, especially in the prominence given to both Mitt Romney and Jon Huntsman in the early primary battles of 2011 and 2012. So the question we really have to ask is what implications are there for a Mormon Republican president?

I wish I could answer that question with unequivocal statements about how the faith of Joseph Smith and Brigham Young would color the decisions of the chief executive of the United States. However, who could have predicted that a Quaker president would extend the war in Vietnam by another five years after his initial election? Predicting the behavior of any person based on their religion is a perilous course to take. Nixon was not the best of Quakers. Anyone who voted for him on the basis of his religion was making a serious mistake. It is certain that anyone voting for—or against—Mitt Romney or any other Mormon candidate is making the same mistake.   But if the atmosphere created by Joseph Smith's focus on wealth, political power, and the godly exaltation of human beings is any indication of how a potential Mormon candidate would act, or what his or her beliefs may be, then a Mormon presidency will at least be entertaining. A president who believes himself to be on the road to godhood, and who believes that the accumulation of wealth is a sign of divine approval, may reflect not only the presumed apotheosis of a man, but the apotheosis of America, and of all that Americans believe about themselves.

It has often been said that America gets the presidents it deserves.

Somebody say "Amen."

FAMOUS MORMONS

In order to demonstrate the influence that the LDS Church has had—directly or indirectly through its membership—it was felt appropriate to append here a list of Mormons who were influential in American politics and culture in the past fifty years or so. As can be seen, Mormons can be found on either side of the Congressional aisle, although in the years since the fall of the Soviet Union there have been a disproportionate number of Mormon conservatives who vote overwhelmingly for GOP candidates. In any event, the following roll call is educational and reveals that any simplistic, "us versus them" equation when it comes to understanding Mormon politics is doomed to fail.

MORMON DYNASTIES

The most famous of the Mormon political dynasties in the past fifty years has been the Romney clan. George Romney ran for the GOP presidential nomination in 1968, and in 2012 Mitt Romney is running for the same. Romneys have been close to the LDS First Presidency for many years, with Marion Romney holding an elder position within the presidency at the time of the Salamander Letter affair. The Romneys trace their lineage to Mormon missionaries who went to Mexico in the late nineteenth century and who had to flee across the border to the United States at the time of the 1910 Mexican Revolution. The Romneys have been largely Republican, but rarely conservative. George Romney was considered too moderate, and some of the same charges have been leveled against Mitt Romney.

But Mormon dynasties are not limited to Republicans. One of the most famous of the Democratic Mormon dynasties is that of the Udalls. Stewart Udall was President Kennedy's Secretary of the Interior; later, Morris "Mo" Udall ran for the Democratic presidential nomination in 1976, where he was defeated by Jimmy Carter. His son Mark Udall is the US Senator from Colorado, and Mo Udall's nephew Tom Udall is the US Senator from the State of New Mexico. To make matters more interesting, the Udalls are cousins of former GOP Senator Gordon H. Smith of Oregon, and current (2012) GOP US Senator from Utah, Mike Lee, who has been endorsed by the Tea Party and who replaced Hughes-linked and Mullen Company owner Bob Bennett as Senator.

MORMON WOMEN

There have been influential women among the political Mormons, as well. Republican Paula Hawkins (1927–2009) was the first—and so far only—female US Senator who was also a member of the LDS Church. She was also the first woman elected to the US Senate (from Florida, in 1980) without having been the wife or daughter of a politician.

Then there is Angela "Bay" Buchanan. This sister of conservative lightning-rod Pat Buchanan—former Nixon speechwriter and a conservative somewhere to the right of Robert Welch—converted to Mormonism, and was the campaign manager for Pat Buchanan's two runs for the GOP presidential nomination in 1992 and 1996.

OTHER FAMOUS MORMONS

We cannot forget the senior US Senator of Utah, Orrin Hatch, who wields tremendous power on Capitol Hill as ranking member of both the Senate Judiciary Committee and the Senate Finance Committee.

And the Huntsmans have already been mentioned, but what has not been discussed is the philanthropic profile of Jon Huntsman Sr., once named as one of *Fortune* magazine's twenty-five most generous Americans, who built a $100 million cancer institute at the University of Utah among his other generous endowments. Not alone among Mormon businessmen, Huntsman is joined by J.W. "Bill" Marriott Jr., the head of the Marriott hotel chain, as well as many other businesses. Incidentally, there have been Mormons at the head of various iconic American enterprises throughout the last thirty years, such as Black & Decker, Ryder, and Iomega. In addition, Stephen R. Covey—the author of the best-selling *The Seven Habits of Highly Effective People*—is a Mormon who publically has opposed same-sex marriage. Other Mormon authors include science-fiction author Orson Scott Card and, of course, Jack Anderson.

Among the spooky Mormons—alongside Robert Bennett and Bill Gay—we find Brent Scowcroft, who was National Security Advisor to the Gerry Ford administration in 1975, and who also served in similar—intelligence-linked—capacities with Presidents George H.W. Bush (National Security Advisor) and George W. Bush (Chairman of the President's Foreign Intelligence Advisory Board).

This brief summary is only an indication of the extent to which Mormons have been visible and influential in American political and cultural life. While it may be difficult to claim with any great degree of certainty the overall agenda of the LDS Church when it comes to America's political future, it seems safe to say that Mormons will continue to exert an influence—both overt and covert—over American life and experience, and that it will not deviate overmuch from the doctrines contained in the Book of Mormon and in the occult and hermetic revelations of Joseph Smith, Jr. The cultural conservatism with which Mormons seem to be associated—their almost boring conformity, blandness, and lack of personal idiosyncracy—may be only a protective coloration, designed to deflect attention away from a history of proxy baptisms, secret endowments, plural marriage, and human divinization that would make them more interesting. After all, as author William Henry has pointed out in his books and videotapes, the central feature of the US Capitol Building in Washington, D.C. is a painting of George Washington on the Capitol dome. It is called the "Apotheosis of Washington" and thus insists that this talismanic American and ultimate Founding Father, military leader, political leader and Freemason, had achieved his own "exaltation." Is that, then, the American Way? Is that what we really believe, not only as Mormons—members of that quintessential American faith—but as American citizens in general?

In fact, this may be the real root of what has been called "American exceptionalism" and if it is, what does that mean for our future as a country? If we are alone among nations in this belief of human perfectibility—the goal, after all, of the Bavarian Illuminati who were first called "Perfectibilists"—then it stands to reason we will always endure the hostility of those nations and peoples and faiths for which the notion of human divinization—of Mormon "exaltation"—is anathema. Is the "clash of civilizations" to be waged between those who believe in a kind of individually-attained spiritual evolution and those who believe that humans can only reach their full potential by surrendering their souls, as a community, to an unseen God?

Mormons believe that they can attain exaltation only through submission to the doctrines and covenants of their faith, thus bridging the gap between individual attainment and organized faith. It is a dangerous bridge to cross, for the path is narrow and unforgiving. Like that between individual freedom, on the one hand, and responsibility to the community on the other. It is a work-in-progress, like that of America itself.

In any case, it will be fun and informative to watch the ongoing tug of war between Mormon doctrines and secrecy, and the goal of American transparency and the associated abridgement of individual freedoms and privacy. It is not only a political struggle, begun all those years ago with Joseph Smith's creation of his own army, his own currency, and his own laws and continuing through Brigham Young's stewardship of the LDS Church and the Great Accommodation, but also a cultural one. This tension between who we are as Americans and who we are as individuals will continue to define us as a nation. And the struggle between religion and politics—between the freedom of religious expression and action, and the freedom of political belief and action—will be the stage on which this dramatic, cosmological drama will be enacted. There are deeper concepts at work here, concepts that represent the unconscious material of the American mind and, by extension, of human experience in general. Religion and politics. God and presidents. Exaltation and redemption.

Spirituality versus materialism. Angels versus sorcerers.

Go back to your seats. The curtain has just been raised on the second act.

RECOMMENDED READING

For those who desire to examine the sources for themselves, there are a number of excellent volumes that go into much further detail than have I in this book. The following is a suggestive and not exhaustive list of the sources I have used to research the subject of Mormonism. For ease of reference, I have divided the sources by their respective chapters.

CHAPTER ONE

The life of Joseph Smith, Jr. can be found in several biographies, most notable among them Fawn Brodie's *No Man Knows My History*. That the biography is not a worshipful one can be judged by the sneering reaction of official Mormondom in an article "debunking" Ms. Brodie, entitled *No Ma'am, That's Not History*. You be the judge.

As for the occult environment in upstate New York at the time the Book of Mormon was received and translated, pride of place must go to D. Michael Quinn's encyclopedic *Early Mormonism and the Magic World View*. Originally written at the time the Salamander Letter was thought to be genuine, it nevertheless exhaustively examines the occult milieu of the time and place of the Book of Mormon and is an excellent guide to the subject. Quinn was eventually excommunicated from the LDS Church, and this book is perhaps the major reason.

Also see Richard Godbeer's *The Devil's Dominion: Magic and Religion in Early New England*, as well as the excellent work by John L. Brooke, *The Refiner's Fire: The making of Mormon Cosmology, 1644–1844*. These works have a lot to say not only about Mormonism, but about America's spiritual heritage in the occult and hermetic works of England and the Continent. These may be read alongside Jon Butler's *Awash in a Sea of Faith: Christianizing the American People*.

CHAPTER TWO

Many of the books cited for Chapter One will be useful as well for Chapter Two, with the possible

addition of *The Mormon Murders* by Steven Naifeh and Gregory White Smith. Also this story is told in more detail in Chapter Eight, the Mark Hofmann scandal is mentioned here first.

CHAPTER THREE

A good source for some of the controversy surrounding the "origins" of the Native American population is *America B.C.* by Barry Fell. While not accepted by most mainstream academics, it nevertheless provides a good overview of the themes introduced by the diffusionists who claim that people from Europe and North Africa visited the east coast of the United States long before Columbus and made their way inland at least as far as the Midwest if not the Arizona and New Mexico.

CHAPTER FOUR

Obviously the best source for the Book of Mormon is the *Book of Mormon* itself. Copies can be found in any library, bookstore, and second-hand bookstore or directly from the LDS Church itself (usually for free). Another resource is the *Church Handbook of Instructions*, published by the LDS Church in 2006, and available online. The Handbook discusses many of the issues covered in this book, including the Endowment ceremonies and "Temple work."

CHAPTER FIVE

Histories of the early years of Mormonism can be found in many places, including on the LDS Church website. Fawn Brodie's biography of Smith, mentioned above, is another good place to start. A great online resource is www.sidneyrigdon.com which boasts a huge collection of newspaper articles from the eighteenth and nineteenth centuries on Mormonism and related subjects.

CHAPTER SIX

For background on the alchemical ideas inherent in Mormonism, interested readers may consult my own *Stairway to Heaven* as well as *The Secret Temple*, which also briefly discusses Mormonism. My *Sinister Forces*, volume one, discusses Joseph Smith and Mormonism as well, and the other volumes in the series examine the role religious and occult ideas have had on American politics.

Also, William Henry has written about apotheosis (the fancy Greek word for "divinization") in a book on the US Capitol Building, *Freedom's Gate: The Lost Symbols in the US Capitol.*

CHAPTER SEVEN

There has been much written concerning the Mountain Meadows Massacre, and attempts by various partisan groups to either whitewash the event or paint it as an official Mormon military action. Most recently, a series of articles in academic publications have tried to analyze the massacre on scientific and archaeological principles. Two of these are worth mentioning and they may be found online. The first is entitled "Mountain Meadows Massacre" and is by Luscinia Brown-Hovelt and Elizabeth J. Himelfarb and can be found at www.archaeology.org/news/mormons.html, and dated November 30, 1999. The other is entitled "A Sight Which Can Never Be Forgotten," by Alyssa Fisher, dated September 16, 2003, and can be found at www.archaeology.org/online/features/massacre. These two articles contain much new information on the Massacre.

CHAPTER EIGHT

Research for this chapter included the book, *The Mormon Murders*, by Steven Naifeh and Gregory White Smith, as well as *Mormon America: the Power and the Promise*, by Richard N. Ostling and Joan K. Ostling.

CHAPTER NINE

Useful material here included *Mormon America*, mentioned above, as well as articles by Michael Barbaro "After a Romney

Deal, Profits and Then Layoffs" in the New York *Times,* November 12, 2011, and Sean Wilentz, "Confounding Fathers: The Tea Party's Cold War Roots" in *The New Yorker,* October 18, 2010. There are a number of useful books on the Howard Hughes empire and the machinations of Chester Davis, Bob Maheu, Bill Gay et al., including *Citizen Hughes,* by Michael Drosnin, *Next to Hughes* by Robert Maheu and Richard Hack, *The Money: the Battle for Howard Hughes's Billions,* by James R. Phelan and Lewis Chester, and even *Hoax: The Inside Story of the Howard Hughes-Clifford Irving Affair,* by Stephen Fay, Lewis Chester and Magnus Linklater, as well as Geoff Schumacher's *Howard Hughes: Power, Paranoia and Palace Intrigue.* The problem with doing any kind of serious research on Hughes is the requirement that one also be conversant with a whole host of related issues, such as the Watergate Affair, E. Howard Hunt, G. Gordon Liddy, Richard Nixon, and so on. Recourse can be had to published documents of the Watergate Hearings as well as the various reports such as the Senate Report on Watergate that the hearings spawned, as well as biographies and autobiographies of the persons involved, from E. Howard Hunt and Gordon Liddy to Hughes, Maheu, Davis, and Nixon (among so many others).

A tremendous resource for researchers interested in everything Mormon is always the Utah Lighthouse Ministry, founded by Jerald and Sandra Tanner. The Tanners were among those who distrusted Mark Hofmann and his forged Mormon documents; at the same time the Utah Lighthouse Ministery is a clearing house for magazines, books, and newsletters on various aspects of Mormonism many of which are written and published by the Ministry itself. They can be found online at www.utlm.org.

Information on Mormon voting patterns is available in several places, notably the Gallup Poll (see the article by Frank Newport entitled "Protestant, Catholic GOP Vote Similar to National Average," dated January 3, 2012, and available at the www.gallup.com website). Also see the forthcoming Georgetown University Press book, *From Pews to Polling Places: Faith and Politics in the American Religious Mosaic,* edited by J. Matthew Wilson and especially Chapter 5, "Dry Kindling: A Political Profile of American Mormons," by David E. Campbell and J. Quin Monson.

CHAPTER TEN

This is the place to advertise my own work, most especially my trilogy on American politics, crime and culture, *Sinister Forces.* The reflections and conjectures in this chapter are the result of decades of study of the American political scene, particularly in its darker aspects, a study that began in the 1970s and which became a series of books beginning with *Unholy Alliance* and extending through *Sinister Forces.*

Some people call this "conspiracy" literature in an attempt to discredit real investigative journalism, which admittedly, has seen better days. Many readers realize that there is something missing in the national dialogue: those intrepid reporters, investigators and journalists who brought us everything from challenges to the Warren Commission to exposure of the Watergate affair. Unfortunately, there are only a few people left who still specialize in this sort of thing (which is startling when one considers how much electronic technology is available today that was not around in 1972). The rest of the field has been surrendered to scare-mongers, red-baiters, and other assorted, if colorful, lunatics. Even what is called "conspiracy" literature has been polarized into left-wing and right-wing conspiracy theorists and even then they are often subsumed under a general heading of "Trust No One," a slogan which is roughly the same as "We Hate Everybody."

Part of the problem is that conspiracy theorists have become spiritualized. All that talk about Bavarian Illuminati and Masonic plots—the stuff of Nazi propaganda as well as of left-wing paranoia—drives the researcher, surrounded by boxes of declassified CIA and FBI documents, a trifle insane. It is so easy to drift from examining one of the Hughes letters from the Romaine Street warehouse heist into a paranoid trance populated by sinister cabals of government sorcerers plotting in Georgetown basements, summoning the Dark Lord. Once you dig beneath the surface of our shared experience of America—with all its mad culture, assassinations, unbelievable political figures, and pounding, mind-numbing multimedia campaigns of pharmaceutical advertising and agit-prop—you come upon a large iron box guarded by some kind of weird transformative reptile. The treasure in that box is not mere filthy lucre; it is the secret of our inheritance, buried there by an English pirate captain, or a Jewish Algonquin rabbi, or a nervous American Freemason. The reptile—toad or salamander, it matters little which—is the sign that we are stumbling in the right direction: down. We have to dig a little deeper, and get a little dirtier, in order to look up with any degree of clarity.

Are there sinister spiritual forces at work in America? Of course, there are. America is a haunted house. Joseph Smith knew that, otherwise why would an Angel have guided the young Sorcerer to a deserted drumlin in the wild American landscape, a territory so many had considered virgin before the arrival of the Pilgrims? Smith knew that the blood of millions of humans had already soaked through the loam and topsoil of upstate New York, that the virginity of this land had been seized long before. He knew that stately pines and maple trees grew from unmarked graves of the ancestors of the human race.

He knew that if there was a truth to be found in the bedrock of America, it was to be found in the susurrating chatter of its ghosts, demons, and angels: speech that can only be heard in its forests, hills and valleys. The spellbooks of the European magicians were written, not for the jaded occultists of France, Germany or England already crowded beyond belief with religions, crusades, inquisitions, witches, and the burnt flesh of heretics, but for the innocent eyes of young believers—heretics themselves—in the world's newest land. For a people who had abandoned the safety of the old and familiar, in search of the new and the possible. These were people who went into the unknown to mold a life from whatever raw material they could find.

Is it any wonder that some went even further into the unknown, into dark temples guarded by unfamiliar watchers? Smith was one of these. For good or ill, as hoax or divine revelation, Smith's foray into the world of spirit and angel was ambitious and pioneering. It was a truly American mission, an ancient drama of gods and prophets and madmen and assassins played out in the New World. It was the insistence that this land, too, is promised. This land, too, is sacred.

No matter what we think of it, no matter what we believe, it is something to watch. I have devoted the three volumes of *Sinister Forces: A Grimoire of American Witchcraft* to the cause of understanding this phenomenon, this purely American spirituality that is part-European, African and Asian on the one side and part indigenous.... something ... on the other. Most Americans have little direct knowledge of Native American culture; most Native Americans have little knowledge about the "Old Ones" who lived on the North and South American continents before their own culture developed. Smith tried to answer that omission by filling the gap with his own wonder, his own imagination, the whisperings of a dead race, an unequalled lust for life ... and a few, well-placed, deceptions.

America. What a concept!

ACKNOWLEDGEMENTS

I will make this short. Not many people in this election year would want to be associated with a book on Mormonism, especially a book that could be interpreted as either promoting the religion (it does not) or attacking it (it does not). The book could also be construed—from a distance—as a "hit piece" on GOP presidential candidate Mitt Romney. It is not that, either. I would prefer if readers assumed that this book was the result of an alien visiting America in January, 2012 and trying to make sense of it.

I come to the study of Mormonism with a jaundiced view, certainly, but also with a sense of awe. The study of Mormonism is the study of religion in general. If there is any point I would like readers to take away from this book, it is that Mormonism is no different from any other religion: it is as far-fetched, illogical, unreasonable, and unscientific as any mainstream faith. And that is as it should be. Who wants a religion based on scientific principles? Who wants to go to their grave praying the Four Laws of Thermodynamics? Religion is about meaning, something that science can never provide.

That said, I would like to acknowledge those who thought that this book might be just the thing to snuggle up to on a cold November evening in an election year.

First, Stuart Weinberg of Seven Stars bookstore in Boston, Massachusetts, who was thinking out loud one day and suggested that a book on Mormonism would be perfect this year, especially after he heard me talk about how both Mormonism and Scientology began with rituals of ceremonial magic based on precisely the same occult texts.

Then, there is Donald Weiser and Yvonne Paglia who supported this endeavor, morally and otherwise.

Then, of course, James Wasserman. I wrote many lines with Jim's voice in the back of my head, warning me to remain nonpartisan and un-biased. You don't want Jim's voice in the back of your head. For that reason, I hope that this book satisfies the partisans of whichever stripe.

Also Michael Kerber and Lisa Trudeau of Red Wheel/ Weiser. We walked together through the process of writing and crafting this book so that it would not be a mere flash-in-the-pan for an election year but a book that would stand the test of time as an in-depth look at the history and doctrines (and practices) of one of our most important American religions.

There are others I can thank, and should thank, but they would probably not want their names to be memorialized here in case their candidate loses! Thus, they can be sure I am remembering them and acknowledging them, and that they will enjoy the fruits of my gratitude in Joseph Smith's celestial realm after their process of divinization has become complete!

Peter Levenda
Florida, 2012